To The Queen...
A Royal Drinkology

To The Queen...
A Royal Drinkology

The Diamond Jubilee
of
Her Majesty Queen Elizabeth II

1952–2012

By

Thomas J.M. Mace Archer DeLacroix-Mills
Secretary General ~ British Monarchist Society

ISBN: 978-0-9572675-0-3

Designed by Aleksander Lenart
Watercolours by Edward Lee Showalter
Edited by Ava Alexandra Dawn
Published by Diamond Rose & Crown Ltd. ~ London, New York, Montreal

Printed by PrintHouse Corporation Ltd. ~ Park Royal, London

Dedication

In dedication to Her Majesty, Queen Elizabeth II

For being the envy of every politician, the heart of a nation, and a role model to many around the world. Here is to 60 glorious years on the throne, and many more to come. We would not be where we are today if it were not for your guidance, care and courage. God Save The Queen!

Authors Acknowledgements

For Betty Mills – *A Grandmother Loved Always*

and for

George Mills – *The most loyal and dutiful Grenadier Grandfather I know.
Thank you for affording me such a fine "Royal" education.*

Special Thanks

To My Families – *For always being supportive, believing in my dreams,
steadying me when I stumble and cushioning my falls.*

To Yvonne D – *Keep Calm, Carry On and Triumph.*

To Carol, Bobby, Tricia & Ava – *For whom this book would not have been.*

Table of Contents

Foreword

Rafe Heydel-Mankoo

Royal Commentator & Editor
Burke's World Orders of Knighthood and Merit

Approximately 80% of the British population has known no Sovereign other than Her Majesty Queen Elizabeth II. Her Majesty's image is the most reproduced in world history and she is arguably the most recognisable person in the world. As the Sovereign of 16 Realms and Head of a Commonwealth of 54 nations representing over one-quarter of the world's population, The Queen is the world's only transnational monarch. She has treated with 12 British Prime Ministers and known 12 American presidents, starting with President Harry S. Truman (President Lyndon Johnson was the only President she did not meet). No other world leader has comparable experience. Her Majesty's 60 year reign exemplifies the very best qualities of constitutional monarchy: stability, tradition and continuity.

Her Majesty's Diamond Jubilee is an occasion for unashamed celebration of the remarkable achievements of both The Queen and her various Realms. Jubilee celebrations are occasions for merriment and entertainment, for parades and parties. Few celebrations feel complete without a libation of some sort. I am therefore delighted that Thomas J. Mace Archer Delacroix-Mills has crafted this practical, informative and entertaining book of royal drink recipes and mementos to celebrate the Diamond Jubilee. It is common knowledge that The Queen enjoys a dubonnet and gin cocktail, as did Her Majesty Queen Elizabeth the Queen Mother, but in this light-hearted and respectful book we are taken on a fascinating historical tour through the wine cellars and drinks cabinets of Britain's royal homes; discovering, on the way, the special tipples preferred by various members of the Royal Family. Whether you choose to celebrate this once-in-a-lifetime milestone with millions in The Mall, at one of the thousands of street parties that will be held across the nation, or privately in your own home, this book will enable you to toast Her Majesty in suitably regal style. And so we should. Over the decades, as the world changes ever more rapidly and dramatically, becoming, in the process, both increasingly chaotic and unfamiliar, The Queen stands as a steadfast symbol of stability and continuity. She grounds us. The familiar sight of Our Sovereign, with her captivating smile and genteel wave, is enough to remind us that some things never change. From this we draw comfort and hope. However, Her Majesty is more than mere constant or symbol of modern history. One need not accomplish anything to attain that status. One need simply exist. No, The Queen is far more. She is human. She is alert to humanity. She is conscious of duty. She is an inspiration.

A healthy and productive society requires role models and icons. Their function is manifold but they ultimately serve to motivate, inspire and guide both the society as well as its constituent parts. Our era, for whatever reason, suffers from a lack of true role models. Real leadership and the notion of justifiably deserved respect and admiration have been all but forgotten in critical areas of modern life, replaced instead by artificially inflated figures of the hour or moment artfully created by powerful corporate hands and posed to resemble the genuine artefact. We are encouraged and expected to idolise and collectively prostrate ourselves before those who have become the physical personification of greed, selfishness and ego; in short, before those for whom "I" has become the all-important mantra and for whom duty is understood only in terms of what others must do for them. Their faces are plastered on bill boards, on magazines, on television and in the cinema. These are the great and powerful we are told. They are to be revered.

All that glitters is not gold. Beside the genuine that which is inflated and artificial looks crude and cheap. The Queen is the real McCoy. She towers over feeble imitations. In a life dominated by personal self-sacrifice, dedication to duty and concern for others, even in the midst of great personal tragedy, Her Majesty epitomises much that is truly noble in the human spirit. To her we can look for examples of strength during adversity and calmness of spirit during times of upheaval. Whilst in almost all other areas society seems to cater to the lowest common denominator how refreshing and inspiring to know that here at least stands a shining example of those deeply cherished values and all-important beliefs that have guided civilised man through the ages. Let us take pride in that fact and revel in the anthem and the prayer: God Save The Queen!

Royal Drinkology

Famed as much for their love of the drink as they are for their prosperous or tumultuous reigns, Britain's Monarchs have always indulged in their favourite choices of ales, liquors and spirits, and Her Majesty Queen Elizabeth II is no exception. No matter who may have reigned at any given time, it was the ancient monarchs who were most notable for enjoying meads, while the court of King Henry VIII was notable for grand wine cellars and barrels of ale. In modern times it has been the consumption of liquors and spirits that have been associated with the drinks of royalty. Queen Victoria's favourite drink was a mixture of claret and single malt whisky, whilst her son King Edward VII enjoyed Iced Champagne. King George V enjoyed his whisky so much that he granted the First Royal Warrant to Johnny Walker and Sons Ltd., to supply whisky to the Royal Household. The Uncrowned King Edward VIII enjoyed anything alcoholic, whilst his dutiful brother King George VI enjoyed his whisky much like his father. The Queen Mother when Duchess of York, was photographed "fishing for Champagne" at a garden party in aid for the Princess Elizabeth Hospital for Children in London.

As events unfolded and the Duke and Duchess of York found themselves as King and Queen of the United Kingdom, it was not just the people who would toast Their Majesties, but Their Majesties whom would often times toast the nation and those around them. The Queen Mother's niece, the Honourable Margaret Rhodes, who was also her Lady-in-Waiting, has described some of Her Majesty's dinners at Birkhall Estate to be "uproarious" in content in which 'At the end of the meal, Queen Elizabeth would start a series of toasts. As well as "Hooray for..." with glasses held high there was even more of "Down with..."' with glasses almost disappearing beneath the table. This example further continues to show that Her Majesty made a point to use spirits as both a token of serious affection and a show of cheeky playfulness when in public and more importantly in the privacy of her own home.

As Queen consort to husband King George VI, it was a Canadian distillery in 1939 that created Crown Royal to honour the State Visit of Their Majesties

Queen Elizabeth and King George VI to Canada in that same year. As Princess Elizabeth became Queen Elizabeth II in 1952 and progressed with her reign, the Queen Mother had a Royal Warrant issued to Gordon's of London to provide Gin to her household at Clarence House, thus rendering Gordon's of London the only Gin maker to hold two simultaneous Royal Warrants: one for Her Majesty Queen Elizabeth II, and the other to Her Majesty, the Queen Mother. Her Majesty, Queen Elizabeth, the Queen Mother enjoyed her Gin often mixing it with tonic or Dubonnet. Upon the death of Her Majesty, floral tributes including bottles of Gin were left in memoriam of this famed Queen who was well-known to have loved her Gin almost as much as she loved her people. According to the Honourable Margaret Rhodes, the Queen's alcohol intake never varies. Following in her mother's footsteps, Her Majesty takes a Gin and Dubonnet before lunch, with a slice of lemon and ice. She will then take wine with her lunch and further enjoy a dry Martini and a glass of champagne in the evening. In light of this calculated and timed consumption of daily alcohol, it can assuredly be said that Her Majesty continues to uphold the family tradition of a right "Royal" drink. As further confirmation of Her Majesty's fondness of a good, relaxing drink, it has often been cited in a well-known exchange over lunch between Queen Elizabeth II and her mother, the late Queen Elizabeth, the Queen Mother, that Elizabeth II stated, "I wonder if I might have a second glass of wine?" to which her mother replied with a smile, "Is that wise? You know you have to reign all afternoon." In light of this uproarious exchange between mother and daughter, it is certain that even Her Majesty feels the pressures of her job, in which she too can relate to the work-related stress of her people. It is almost assured that these pressures and stresses associated with her position often lead Her Majesty to an extra drink on some days of the week.

Like his predecessors and their consorts, it will be Prince William and the Duchess of Cambridge who will continue the long line of royal association with spirits. His Royal Highness, the Prince William and Her Royal Highness, Catherine,

Duchess of Cambridge have already shown that they have a preference in their drink. Prince William favours a "Crack Baby Cocktail", which mixes fresh passion fruit with vodka and champagne whilst the Duchess prefers an association with whisky (much like the reigning sovereigns of old) which she sips slowly.

Our very own "Party Prince" Harry indulges in a plethora of spirits and ales when on the town with friends, however he prefers a very high quality Vodka which can cost well over £1,000 per bottle. Most recently on his tour of Belize on Her Majesty's service, Prince Harry could be seen delighting in local Rums which according to his facial expressions were of a much higher proof than expected. Younger members of our extended Royal family also have their favourite tipples as Princess Beatrice has shown the nation on various occasions; enjoying such refreshments as cider at Wimbledon and a plethora of hard liqueur cocktails on girls' nights out with her Mother (the former Duchess of York). Reports have shown Princess Beatrice to have "out-drank" her cousins Princes William and Harry moving her into the newly-acquired title of "Party Princess". Out-drinking her royal counterparts show that this York can truly hold her own when partaking in a right royal consumption of spirits, though the press photos prove otherwise.

As lager and ales have proven to be a staple of Prince Philip and several of the grandchildren, Her Majesty has extended her interest in the brew by visiting several breweries and distilleries over her reign. She has most recently visited the Guinness brew house while on her first-ever State visit to Ireland in May of 2011. As she and Prince Philip toured the facility, a freshly-pulled pint was placed in front of her on a bar. She kindly smiled and stepped back whilst Prince Philip could be seen to want to indulge in the delight of a nice pint as he rocked back and forth toward the foaming drink before finally backing slowly away. Though Prince Philip's favourite brew is Boddingtons, one could see the smile on his face and the look of desire in his eye as the pint of Guinness sat lonely on the bar top. As the fresh pint beckoned him like a child to a sweet shop, one can be assured that a younger member of the Windsor family would not have been able to just walk away without tasting the soft creamy foam on their lips.

The younger members of our Royal family are no exception when it comes to 'downing a few' in times of relaxation and/or celebration. As the younger generations of Windsors (both Prince and Princess alike) partake in the vibrant and colourful night-life of the various clubs and pubs of our capital city, as well as the places in which they travel to and holiday in; we can always count on the drink as being a steadfast friend. Late evenings and early mornings of stumbling to the motor, or playing in a fountain which has been caught by the paparazzi have no doubt shown us just how friendly the drink is to our Royals but no harm, no foul when we are having fun coming into our own. Royal or not, we all have enjoyed forgetting ourselves every now and again with our intoxicating friend and it is with respect to our friend the drink that we all can share the same altering experience no matter our station in life.

No matter whether in public or private, at sea in a boat, on land in a train, in a Palace or rustic Deeside cottage, the royal family each has their own distinct drink of choice. No matter the occasion, spirits are always at the forefront of any form of entertaining when associating with the Queen and her family. Family gatherings such as Christmas at Sandringham see a multitude of drinks being consumed amongst the Royal Family. As this is the first year that the newly-married Duchess of Cambridge is entering the world of holidays with the Queen and her Family, we are sure to see her lift her glass more than once when gathering together with her royal counterparts as they sip on their Gin and Tonics. Dry Martinis are the chosen Christmas Eve drinks for Her Majesty, Prince Philip and Prince Charles when at Sandringham, whilst Gin and tonic is served in frigid abundance to the rest of the family. This past Christmas not only saw new members of the family entering the fold but it was the first time in decades that Her Majesty has invited such a large gathering of Windsors to her Norfolk country estate. A total of 27 members of

her family had been invited and the lack of sufficient room to comfortably fit all of the guests led to the lesser members of the family being accommodated in the servants' quarters during their stay. This fact alone would most certainly be cause to have a drink or three whilst Her Majesty prepared her home for the arrival of her immediate and extended family on this most historic of Christmas holidays.

It is not just during family gatherings or at holiday times that we see corks being popped and spirits being poured amongst the Royals, this activity is more highly-concentrated during formal functions of State when the Queen is entertaining. State entertaining and formal banquets always begin with toasts to Her Majesty and the visiting Head of State, followed by large quantities of delectable delights, each course being accompanied by a different blend of wine or spirit. Over 20,000 people are entertained annually at exceptional receptions and banquets in which the Queen offers her very best in alcoholic refreshment to her guests. This form of entertaining does not include the extra 30,000 invitees that are entertained by Her Majesty at a number of alcohol-free garden parties. In fact Her Majesty has had approximately 2 million people to tea during her reign.

Cocktail receptions by the hundreds have been held over the last sixty years, in which thousands of bottles of champagnes, wines and ports have been served. Her Majesty's collection of wines, ports and champagnes is amongst the best, if not the best in the world. The cellars themselves are over 300 years of age, some of which were original to Buckingham House, when owned by the Duke of Buckingham before it was bought by King George III, and it then became the official residence of British sovereigns on the accession of Queen Victoria. Worth over £2 Million, the numerous bottles that are kept here in these ancient cellars are kept under the protective and watchful eye of the Yeoman of the Royal Cellars. Totalling a staggering 25,000 bottles, the job of keeping these bottles in the perfect environment is quite difficult, as there are seven large vault-like rooms that comprise the royal cellars. Such valuable bottles stored here include a Sherry dating from 1660 as well as "newer" wines such as Château Léoville Barton 1988, Château Chasse Spleen 1990, Château Batailley 1994, Château Latour à Pomerol 1995, Château Fonroque 1995, Château Beau-Site 1995, Nuits St. Georges 1996, as well as Château Meyney 1996, which are housed together with South African Chardonnays and New Zealand Sauvignon Blancs. These rare and vintage wines give way to a variety of exclusive ports such as 1963 Fonseca and Quinta Do Noval. It is not only the wine cellars at Buckingham Palace that hold such rarities and bottles of value, as it can be assumed that each of the residences that are inhabited by Her Majesty, undoubtedly hold a plethora of such alcoholic treasures. No matter where the Queen may entertain, be it formal or informal, we can rest assured that nothing but the finest of alcohols is being served. Even whilst the Queen and royal family are "off duty" and away at Balmoral for their private summer holiday, the bottles still pop and the spirits flow like the River Dee.

It is not always in time of celebration, or State occasioning that the drink is used in and around the royal family. It is often used in times of despair to relieve the stresses of public life for those such as in the case of the late King Edward VIII during and after the abdication crisis. King George VI and Queen Elizabeth each calmed their nerves during the blitz and after long walkabouts where they surveyed the damage left by the bombs of WWII. Prime Minister Winston Churchill was known to always have a drink with his cigar, and in Prime Minister Tony Blair's case, it was used to escape a less than entertaining annual visit to meet the Queen in Scotland during his time at 10 Downing Street. Tony Blair was able to keep his wits about him whilst visiting Her Majesty on the annual Balmoral weekend, where Her Majesty extends her hospitality to the current Prime Minister and his wife each year for a weekend of rustic retreat at her private Castle. Not known for their love of the wilderness or their less than luxurious lifestyle, the Blairs found this annual weekend to be quite trying and not in line with their own personal expectations of grandeur.

Quoted from his autobiography Tony Blair stated that: "Using the bathroom on the other side of the corridor was a singular act of courage, sneaking open the bedroom door, glancing right and left and then making for it at speed". This quote really illustrates his resentment for the lack of en suite fixtures one would have whilst staying at the Ritz or newly-renovated Savoy. However 'Tony' and his wife Mrs. Blair were not at the Ritz, nor were they checked in at the Savoy, they were guests of Her Majesty at her private home where one would be honoured just to be considered for this most coveted of invitations and would be delighted to make do with what was available at the Queen's private castle. Coping with the less than luxurious surroundings, Blair looked forward to the abundant drinks that he described as "rocket fuel" which helped him survive the weekend. These drinks helped him relax, to the point which he described as, "The burden and the head got lighter". Knowing the relationship between "just call me Tony" and Her Majesty...it is surely speculated that the Queen needed her drink just as much as the Blairs needed theirs on this most uncomfortable of annual visits. Thank the good Lord that for every occasion, good or bad, of ease or stress we can always turn to the drink to celebrate a right royal celebration or dreaded encounter!

This compilation of "Royal" drink recipes is enhanced with mixers of writings, poems, quotes and fun facts about Her Majesty to create a truly unique and specially blended book experience to celebrate not just the Mother of our Nation, but a woman who is near and dear to many the world over. It is on our ships at sea, in our outposts around the world and at our dinner tables at home, that the familiar and endearing toast "to the Queen!" has been followed with nothing less than a spirit of our own choosing.

Many a book has been written and published about this famed Stateswoman, but on such a rare and special occasion as a Diamond Jubilee, it is only fitting that a book as unique as the celebration itself be made. As the Head of State of 16 nations and the Leader of the Commonwealth of 54 nations, Her Majesty has made quite a mark on the world stage in her 60 years as Queen. In times of both good and bad, it was Elizabeth II who celebrated with and comforted her people. She has been the beacon of hope and light in dark days as well as the beaming example of how we as individuals and as a society should be.

It is not for her legend that we celebrate on the occasion of this Diamond Jubilee, it is for the person she is, and the unforgiving duty that she has carried out without complaint or blemish for the past 60 years. More than just a Queen, this daughter, sister, wife, mother, grandmother, aunt, and niece did not apply for the job she currently has, a job for life she never asked for and a burden that would see most, aged and immobile at her spry age, is something that Her Majesty does not take lightly. She dedicated her whole life to our service in which she has served her people and nation in a manner that has brought renewed popularity to the Institution of Monarchy and renewed worldwide fame and respect to not only her Kingdoms and realms but the Commonwealth too.

Her face has changed little over sixty years, as it is still the most recognised face no matter which portion of the planet you inhabit. At one time she was a princess without the pressures of the world on her shoulders. She was a newly-wed wife and in love with a changing world and its people. It was in a far away and exotic land that she had her title of Princess stripped away as she returned to her native country as Queen to just about one-third of the world's population. As the sun never set on the British Empire, it has not yet set on the face of this young and energetic woman who was thrust into the world of Statesmanship at the tender and young age of 25. It was a solemn day when her father, King George VI passed, a day on which she was truly and unmistakably bound for her entire life to not only her nation and its people but the territories and realms over the seas that hailed her accession to the world's most famous throne. As she arrived home and disembarked the plane onto the tarmac at London Airport, this young gentle wife and mother in mourning, held the poise of a formidable Queen as she was greeted by her first Prime Minister Winston Churchill and an entourage of statesmen. Who was to know that after this sad homecoming the woman who left a Princess (seen for the very last time by her father as he waved goodbye to her at London Airport) and returned a Queen would in fact come to span one of the longest and most successful reigns that our rain-soaked and windswept isles have ever seen.

As the months, weeks and days of 60 years have passed, so has the world and the nations in which she has reigned over. During her reign, the majority of the world's population was born for she has been the only Queen most of us have ever known our entire lives. She has been there with us during every major event that has happened in our lives and continues to be the one constant that we can always look to as a source of fairness, light and example as she herself is the culmination of unbiased love, strong values and tolerance. Her reign has spanned six Archbishops and six Popes, 13 British, 11 Canadian, 12 Australian and 14 New Zealand Prime Ministers. 12 United States President's have sat in office since she became Queen as well as a further nine Prime Ministers from Jamaica, seven from Barbados, St. Lucia and Papua New Guinea, three from the Bahamas, eight from Grenada, 10 from the Solomon Islands, four from St. Vincent and the Grenadines, and Belize, 12 from Tuvalu, three from Antigua and Barbuda and two from St. Kitts and Nevis. Her Majesty has had a total of 153 Prime Ministers during her reign, 30 of which are Prime Ministers from former Commonwealth realms. Some of her realms and territories have sought true freedom in the form of independence from the crown while others still remain as entrusted to her as they were the day she became Queen.

Throughout the second-longest reign in British history, nations have fallen, as new ones have emerged, great celebrations as well as great tragedies have occurred, the state of the world once teetered on the brink of nuclear war, and the doomsday scenario of the millennium came and went. Great leaders in politics and religion have been born and others have died as the natural face of our planet has changed tremendously since 1952. No matter what has happened in our lives, for better or for worse, the one true constant that has always been, is Her Majesty, The Queen. In this year of great celebration it is a true honour to say we have lived in a new and modern Elizabethan era – a marvel to be able to say we have lived during the time of Elizabeth II. God Save The Queen!

Royal Gin Drinks

I have taken more good out of alcohol than alcohol has ever taken from me.

Winston Churchill (1874-1965)
British Politician, Statesman and Prime Minister

Gin is a much-loved drink of not only the British people, but their Royal Family. Closely related to the continental Genever, both alcohols are clear in nature and infused with juniper berries and an assorted bouquet of herbs and spices. It is composed mainly from rye or wheat due their durability long after the growing season is over. Gin is naturally light-bodied and refreshing whereas Genever is comprised of a mixture of wheat, corn, rye and malted barley which makes for a heartier alcohol similar in part to a stronger and more boldly-flavoured malt whisky. As the distillation is the deciding factor to the potency and flavour of the Gin, it is the assortment of the ingredients such as Juniper and other additives consisting of, but not limited to, Anise, Angelica Root, Cinnamon, Orange Peel, Coriander and Cassia Bark to name a few which contribute to this. Initially distilled in column stills, it is the clean process of distillation which sees very little additives of congers and flavouring agents to the mixture of Gin which results in a distinct proof and flavour of the alcohol. However, each distillery has their own distinct recipe for the creation of this most refreshing and lighter of spirits.

The quality of Gin is often related to its unique number of distillations, which is directly accredited to the final process of distilling in which high quality Gins are distilled and re-distilled several times. It is during the final process of this unique art of spirit-making where distilling is suspended for certain amounts of time that allows the Gin (alcohol) vapours to proceed through a calculated and specialised motion. This component of distilling allows the alcohol to absorb the flavour of the oils and compounds of the specially blended bouquet of juniper berries and other elements on its short journey to the distillery condenser which flavours this world-class spirit to a very distinct flavour and complex composition. Gin has a varied degree of complexity and composition, in which this fine spirit is widely categorised through different recipes and distilling processes. Types of Gin include Plymouth Gin, Old Tom Gin and Genever or Hollands Gin, which is the Dutch style of this famed spirit. London Dry Gin is the most popular and highly demanded English recipe not only in Britain but our former colonies, including America and oddly enough Spain. It is known to be light on the palate and popular for mixing. Britain produces mostly dry Gin, primarily from the column still form of distilling, in which our Gins tend to be of high proof (90° or 45% ABV) with a very distinct bouquet composed of citrus from the use of dried lemon and Seville orange peels. Spain produces a substantial amount of Gin in the London Dry style which is true to the column still form of distilling.

The origins of Gin in Britain can be traced back to their Majesties William and Mary of Orange. Upon assuming the highly coveted throne of England after the Glorious Revolution, King William (a Protestant) set forth a series of laws and taxes to hinder the importation of wines and spirits from Catholic nations, most importantly Brandy. In knowing a substitute for the less available spirits would be needed, the King encouraged spirits to be made from readily available and local products such as grains of wheat and rye, whilst reducing and eventually eliminating taxes and fees on replacement spirits such as Gin. Gin has remained popular and at the forefront of British spirit consumption throughout the centuries not only at home, but abroad. During the days when the sun never set on the British Empire, never did it cast a shadow on the vats of Gin that accompanied our travels. Exporting to and eventually distilling in every corner of the globe that we explored, Gin was the preferred drink of choice. Though the Caribbean saw a sharp rise in Rum consumption and exportation, Gin was the steadfast friend of the colonies and eventually the Empire.

As the classifications of Gin were challenged and categorised, it was London Dry that triumphed over all others. It was during the time of Queen Victoria that Gin entered its extreme height of popularity which saw Gin being consumed in great quantities. Ladies sipped their Gins whilst planning their social diaries, as our men in uniform practically bathed in the hundreds of newly- found drink recipes that would see Gin as the main component. Gin was also not excluded from the medical field by any means, as it was during this time that the ever-constant Gin and Tonic water (which contains quinine – a medicine used to treat malaria) was introduced to the tropical colonies as a way to combat and slow the spread of malaria, rather than consuming the foul-tasting and elusive bitterness of quinine alone. Without doubt, the best-known Gin mixed drink is the Martini. This mixture of only 2 parts Gin to 1 part White Vermouth found its niche in the late 19th century, and has been the drink mostly associated with the stories of luxury and grandeur of the times, but do not be fooled that the Martini is a drink of a bygone era, as it is still very popular amongst many social circles today.

Thomas' Jubilee Gin with a Twist

Gin
Tonic (*of a 'Dry Canadian' nature*)
1 lime
1 lemon

Thomas's very own twist on a classic British summer staple. As Thomas prefers not to formally measure but to judge his pouring, the above ingredients are freely used. In a short rocks glass filled with ice, pour the Tonic 1/4 of the way up the glass. Muddle one half of a lime and of a lemon and pour in the juices (this should bring you almost to 1/2 the glass, if not add a little more Tonic and juice), pour in your Gin (I count until about '3' or until the glass is 85% full) then top off with Tonic. Swizzle the cocktail until properly mixed and enjoy. You have never had better summer refreshment. I use the above-referenced tonic as it is sweeter in nature, which balances out the Gin and citrus, creating a very smooth and light drink which is certain to help your summer pass by enjoyably.

FUN FACT

At the age of 13 Princess Elizabeth met, and was immediately smitten by, her future husband, now the Duke of Edinburgh.

QUOTE

"What were once only hopes for the future have now come to pass; it is almost exactly 13 years since the overwhelming majority of people in Ireland and Northern Ireland voted in favour of the agreement signed on Good Friday 1998, paving the way for Northern Ireland to become the exciting and inspirational place that it is today".

Queen Elizabeth II

1 oz ≈ 30 ml

Traditional British Gin and Tonic

FUN FACTS

Her Majesty is a long-time devotee of Hermes scarves – the ultimate status-symbol scarf that's been worn by Grace Kelly and Hillary Clinton.

The Queen is the only person in Britain who can drive without a licence or a registration number on her car. And she doesn't have a passport.

2 oz Gin
5 oz Tonic water
1 lime wedge
1 lemon wedge

In a short rocks glass, fill with ice, pour tonic followed by Gin into the glass. Follow with fruit wedge and stir with your favourite swizzle stick for a cool and refreshing cocktail. Serve and enjoy. Repeat these steps as often as desired.

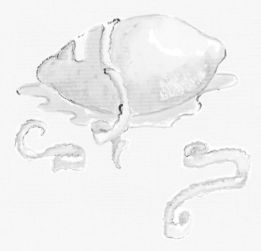

HM Queen Elizabeth Martini

1/2 oz Dry Vermouth
1 1/2 oz Gin
1 1/2 tsp Benedictine herbal liqueur

Stir all ingredients in a shaker or posh glass pitcher with ice, strain into a cocktail glass and serve with a green olive. If preferred, shake in shaker until your hands hurt from the cold and then pour into a chilled Martini glass for a frothy refreshing feel. Raise your full glass and proclaim: "To the Queen" – a toast to her health!

FUN FACTS

Her Majesty has given regular Tuesday evening audiences to 12 British Prime Ministers. Her first Prime Minister being Winston Churchill 1951-55.

Her Majesty is 5ft 4 inches or 160cm tall.

1 oz ≈ 30 ml

Lord of Mann

Also known as Royal Gin Fizz

2 oz Gin
juice of 1/2 a lemon
1 tsp powdered sugar
1 egg
carbonated water

In a shaker, shake all ingredients (except carbonated water) with ice and strain into a highball glass over two ice cubes. Fill with carbonated water, stir, serve and enjoy the experience which can only be expressed as a right royal peculiar.

Queen's Crush

Also known as Dubonnet Royal

1 oz Dubonnet Rouge Vermouth
1/2 oz Gin
2 dashes Bitters
2 dashes Curacao Orange Liqueur
1 dash Pastis liqueur

Stir (or shake vigorously for a fully mixed and frothy cocktail) all ingredients in a shaker with ice, strain into a cocktail glass over ice, serve, savour and enjoy.

FUN FACT

The Queen has sent more than 280,000 telegrams to couples in the UK and the Commonwealth celebrating their diamond wedding (60 years) anniversary.

QUOTE

"The lessons from the peace process are clear; whatever life throws at us, our individual responses will be all the stronger for working together and sharing the load."

Queen Elizabeth II

1 oz ≈ 30 ml

Court of St James

Also known as Piccadilly Cocktail

FUN FACTS

In 2002 (at 76 years of age) the Queen was the oldest monarch to celebrate a Golden Jubilee. The youngest was James I (James VI of Scotland) at 51 years of age.

As a young girl, The Queen and her sister, Princess Margaret acted in a number of Pantomimes during World War Two including playing the part of Prince Florizel in Cinderella in 1941. These pantomimes took place every year in the Waterloo Chamber at Windsor Castle.

1 dash Absinthe
1 dash Grenadine
1/3 part French Vermouth
2/3 part Dry Gin

In a shaker filled with ice, pour all ingredients into the shaker and shake well (I prefer to stir, as shaking bruises the alcohol) strain into a cocktail glass with ice, and garnish with a cherry and lime wheel. After several of these drinks the lights of any room will be a reflection of Piccadilly Circus.

Buckingham Palace

Also known as Imperial Martini

1 oz Dry Vermouth
2 oz Gin
1 tsp Maraschino Liqueur
lemon twist for garnish

Stir all ingredients in a shaker or posh glass pitcher with ice, strain into a cocktail glass, and serve with a green olive and lemon twist. If preferred, shake in the shaker and remember to wear your winter gloves, and then pour into chilled Martini glass for a frothy cool feel.

FUN FACT

Queen Elizabeth II is the fortieth monarch since William the Conqueror obtained the crown of England in 1066.

QUOTE

"I have been aware all the time that my peoples, spread far and wide throughout every continent and ocean in the world, were united to support me in the task to which I have now been dedicated with such solemnity."

Queen Elizabeth II

1 oz ≈ 30 ml

Windsor Castle

Also known as Polo Cocktail

1 oz Gin
1 tbsp lemon juice
1 tbsp orange juice

Pour all ingredients in a shaker with ice and shake vigorously to make frothy, strain into a cocktail glass, and serve with an orange slice.

Grenadier Guard

Also known as London Cocktail

2 oz Gin
1/2 tsp Maraschino Liqueur
2 dashes Orange Bitters
1/2 tsp powdered sugar
1 twist lemon

Stir (or shake vigorously for a fully mixed and frothy cocktail) all ingredients in a shaker with ice, strain into a cocktail glass with ice, serve with a lemon twist and savour the flavour.

QUOTE

"It is a job for life, most people have a job and then they go home, and in this existence the job and the life go on together because you can't really divide it up. The boxes and the communications just keep on coming...I'm lucky I am a quick reader".

Queen Elizabeth II

1 oz ≈ 30 ml

Coldstream Guard

Also known as Pall Mall Cocktail

QUOTE

*"I have behind me not only
the splendid traditions and
the annals of more than
a thousand years but the
living strength and majesty
of the Commonwealth and
Empire; of societies old and
new; of lands and races
different in history and
origins but all, by God's Will,
united in spirit and in aim."*

Queen Elizabeth II

1 1/2 oz Gin
1/2 oz Sweet Vermouth
1/2 oz Dry Vermouth
1/2 oz white Crème De Cacao

Stir the gin together with the Vermouths and Crème De Cacao
in an old-fashioned glass half-filled with ice cubes, and serve
plain. I often rim the glass with sugar to enhance this already
sweet treat to satisfy my sweet tooth.

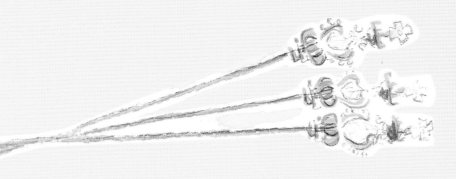

Irish Guard

Also known as London Fog Cocktail

1 1/2 oz London Dry Gin
1/4 oz Pernod

Add the ingredients to a mixing glass filled with ice and stir well. Strain into a chilled cocktail glass and serve with a lime rind. After imbibing a few of these, the fog will certainly set in.

FUN FACT

The Queen is patron of more than 620 charities and organisations.

QUOTE

"I have in sincerity, pledged myself to your service, as so many of you are pledged to mine. Throughout all my life and with all my heart I shall strive to be worthy of your trust."

Queen Elizabeth II

1 oz ≈ 30 ml

The Queen has herself, personally, held over 540 Investitures and has met approximately 4 million people face to face.

Technically, Her Majesty owns all of the sturgeons, whales and dolphins in the waters surrounding the UK. This is due to a statute from 1324 under the reign of King Edward II which states: "Also the King shall have ... whales and sturgeons taken in the sea or elsewhere within the realm." This statute is still valid today and sturgeons, porpoises, whales and dolphins are recognised as 'Fishes Royal'. When captured within three miles of UK shores or washed ashore either dead or alive, they may be claimed on behalf of the Crown. Generally, when brought into port, a sturgeon is sold in the usual way and the purchaser, as a gesture of loyalty, requests the honour of its being accepted by The Queen.

God Save Our Gracious Queen

Also known as Princes Grin Cocktail

2 oz Gin
1 oz apple juice
1 oz apricot nectar
1/2 tsp fresh lemon juice

Stir (or shake vigorously for a fully mixed and frothy cocktail) all ingredients in a shaker with ice, strain into a cocktail glass with ice, serve with a lemon wheel or rind and enjoy. This refreshing cocktail is sure to see a happy grin on your face.

Long To Reign Over Us

Also known as Princes Smile Cocktail

2 oz Gin
1 oz apple juice
1 oz Apricot Brandy
1/2 tsp lemon

Stir (or shake vigorously for a fully mixed and frothy cocktail) all ingredients in a shaker with ice, strain into a cocktail glass with ice, serve with a lemon wheel or rind and enjoy. You will be all smiles after repeating the aforementioned steps several times within a few hours.

FUN FACTS

During her reign, the Queen has journeyed on over 256 official overseas visits to 129 different countries.

The Queen has a bank account at Coutts & Co. There is a Coutts cash-dispensing machine in Buckingham Palace.

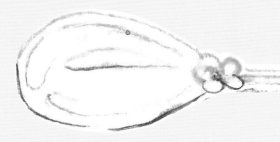

1 oz ≈ 30 ml

The Crown Jewels

Also known as Jewel Cocktail

1 oz Gin
1 oz Green Chartreuse
1 oz Sweet Vermouth
2 dashes Orange Bitters
1 cherry

In a shaker or pitcher stir all ingredients and pour over ice in a small rocks glass. Garnish with cherry. This cocktail is smooth yet refined, a tribute to our Queen who has remained timeless through the years.

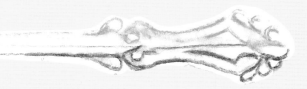

The Commonwealth

Also known as Empire Cocktail

1 1/2 oz Gin
1/2 oz Apple Brandy
1/2 oz Apricot Brandy

Pour all ingredients in a shaker with ice and shake vigorously to make frothy, strain into a cocktail glass, and serve with an orange slice. If you are feeling posh, simply strain into a chilled Martini glass and garnish with a lemon rind.

1 oz ≈ 30 ml

The Royal Cuppa

Also known as Dubonnet and Gin

1/3 Gin
2/3 Dubonnet
lemon

In a tall thin glass place lemon wheel under cubes of ice and pour in the spirits. Simply enjoy this favourite of not only Her Majesty the Queen Mother, but Her Majesty Queen Elizabeth, The Diamond Queen.

Martini

3 oz Gin
1/2 oz Dry Vermouth
1 green olive

Pour all of the ingredients (except the olive) into a shaker almost filled with ice. Shake vigorously and strain into a chilled Martini glass. Garnish with an olive and enjoy this most classic and famous of Gin drinks. It is what we British are known for.

1 oz ≈ 30 ml

Our Diamond Queen

A Poem of Thanksgiving
Written in Honour of Her Majesty's Diamond Jubilee 2012

By

Thomas J. M. Mace Archer DeLacroix Mills

In most nations, leaders come and leaders go
But on the world stage you are still producing our show
Something unique is happening as you continue your life-long reign
As you have brought your Britain home, to renewed world fame
The sudden loss of a king only healed and mended with time
Has lead to a reign celebrated and jubilantly marked with this rhyme
The decades have been filled with much excitement, celebration and loss
That whoever would have thought, a travelling princess would return as boss
A long time indeed it has been, since the year nineteen fifty-two
Starting out as separate entities within our nation, it is together that we grew
A Queen to her people in the beginning, always kept out of range
But over the last many decades there has been a noticeable change
No matter where you go, what you say, or what you do
You are the only one that the world's leaders rightfully bow to
Possessing unthinkable know-how and the deepened skills of State
You have been bound to Britain and its people, for us a most fortunate fate
A superior stateswoman who has more than changed with the times
Means everything to this island nation of deep-rooted history and cockney rhymes
Over Sixty years of the unexpected, you have always been ready
To us your people, always constant, formidable, absolute and steady
Seen as more than an icon, there is not one who does not know your face
But it is no longer for your beauty, your style or your integral grace
You have set forth the example of how we as a society should be
And it is with your help and understanding that we have been kept free
Decades of time you have dedicated to us your people
Never complaining about defending our laws or that cross on the steeple
Most things have changed drastically from what you once knew
But we as a people are especially lucky and blessed to have you

You have always given us everything you have had to give

And still you continue for us, your one and only life to live

Always asking so much of you, you expect very little in return

We can only say thank you by letting the celebratory beacons burn

The envy of the world – you are God's true gift that we possess

As Britain would not be where it is today, if it were not you in that coronation dress

For as long as most of us can remember you have always been there

The mother of our nation – we are ever grateful to have been entrusted to your care

From you over time, we have taken many things away

But never have you been spiteful or changed the rules by which to play

Decommissioning your one true escape and forsaking your beloved boat

We can only begin to make up for it by crafting you a new Jubilee float

Undeserving we are of someone with your values so fair

We celebrate your love with cannons and fireworks in air

No matter what we have done, you have always displayed unconditional love

That to truly reign over us, it must take a lot of help from above

Despite the differences and the events that we have worked through

Never once were we meaning to mishandle or disrespect you

With the time that you have given and the hard work you continue to do

Let it be known the world over that Britain respects, loves and treasures you

Though selfish in a way we may want to be, we cannot forget the Commonwealth

So from all of your people throughout the world we toast your lasting health

Six decades have passed and surely we would ask for sixty years more

As the heart, the soul and the voice of this nation, what more could we ask for

This is the time for great celebration as this year is of course a milestone Jubilee

And as our British history reveals, this time around for you makes three

Celebrating the year with diamonds instead of sparkling silver or shining gold

It is your story of the past sixty years that always and forever will be told

In the years to come, together we have so much more to explore
That with you directing our story we are safe not knowing what's in store
You have served your people proud and are everything that we should be
And as a nation under one crown it is another similar occasion we expect to see
We cannot thank you enough for everything that you have done
And we hope that this year will be one of exceptional fun
Thank you for the memories, the guidance and how over the world we have been seen
As there is no nation luckier than Britain, for you are our Queen!
Happy Diamond Jubilee Year, Your Majesty!
God Save The Queen!

Royal Whisky Drinks

A glass of whisky in Scotland in the thirties cost less than a cup of tea.

Catherine Helen Spence (1825-1910)
Scottish Author, Teacher, Journalist, Suffragette

"To Friar John Cor, by order of the King, to make aqua vitae VIII bolls of malt". Exchequer Rolls 1494-95, vol x, p.487. The Scotch Whisky Association has officially stated that the beginnings of whisky distillation is undetermined, however, it is known that the distillation of a similar spirit was performed by the ancient Celts. This Celtic spirit, known as the "water of life" eventually evolved into a form of Whisky. It has come to be known that the distilling of Whisky became prominent in the 11th century at early Christian Monastic sites. The distilling of spirits remained uninterrupted until 1644 when the Crown levied taxes on Whisky production. The levying of such taxes resulted in outrage amongst the public which led people to take matters into their own hands by illegally distilling their own spirits.

King James IV of Scotland (r. 1488-1513) was known to have a keen liking for Whisky and granted a monopoly for the distillation of Whisky to the Association of Surgeon Barbers. At this time most of the distilling was accomplished by that of the Monks in monasteries, however, it was during the years between 1536 and 1541 that King Henry VIII of England dissolved them thus forcing Whisky production into private homes and farms. During this time, distillation was fairly young in regard to the primitive process of distilling. The Whisky was not matured and often drank as soon as it was distilled thus resulting in a very raw and harsh taste on the palate. It was not until the discovery by accident, when a person was dared to drink Whisky from a forgotten cask, that Whisky was discovered to be more smooth and easier on the palate the longer it was aged. Learning and perfecting distillation, the Old Bushmills Distillery is often credited with being the oldest distillery in the world, as it has maintained its distilling license since 1608.

The Act of Union which united the Crown and lands of England and Scotland in 1707 saw a sharp rise in the tax of Whisky. The English Malt Tax of 1725 saw most of the distillation of Whisky in Scotland dissolved and transformed into an underground movement. To avoid the excise men, the people of Scotland often hid their spirits under altars and in coffins so as to elude the government's representatives. As of the year 1780, there were counted a total of eight legal distilleries, in which a total number of 400 illegal distilleries tilted the scales. Knowing of this gross number of illegal distilleries, parliament passed an excise tax which lead to the easement of restrictions in legal distilleries which made it harder for the illegal production of whisky to remain profitable. The Excise Act, along with the introduction of a new distilling process in 1831 (the end result of the Coffey distillation process, is a whisky that is more smooth than before); and the destruction of wine and cognac production in France during the 1880 Phylloxera Bug helped boost the popularity of Whisky. As Whisky's popularity heightened, even the colonists in America could not turn a blind eye to its station. It was during the war of American Rebellion that Whisky was used as currency and was also traded as a coveted commodity. Until a tax was levied against it Whisky was king in the eyes of the newly created American States. Between the years 1789 and 1794 tensions rose and the Whisky Rebellion took shape which climaxed in 1794 when over 500 people savagely attacked the fortified home of the American tax inspector. The taxes were eventually repealed in 1801.

Whisky is consumed all over the world but it is mostly produced only in grain-growing areas. Just like the people who consume it, not all Whisky is the same. There are many factors that set Whisky apart from other Whiskies such as alcohol content, the base product and the quality of the product. For example, Malt Whisky is made from malted barley whereas Grain Whisky is made from any type of grain. Blended Malt Whisky is comprised of a single malt from different distilleries, whereas Pure Malt or Malt Whisky is nine times out of ten pure vatted, which was formerly termed Vatted Malt Whisky. Single Malt Whisky is from one distillery that only uses one type of grain. If Single Malt Whisky is described as a single cask Whisky, it will contain Whisky from several casks of different years so that it will enhance the flavour and taste of the batch and so also identifies which distillery it is from. The most notable of the distilleries that uses this method and also indicate the processes associated with their certain distilling and maturing in a port wine cask are Bushmills, Nikka, and The Glenlivet. Whiskies that are known to be Blended Whiskies are often made by mixing malt and grain Whisky together with flavourings and caramel colouring. The Whiskies that are simply described as Canadian, Irish or Scotch are certain to be blended Whiskies which are from several distilleries so they are distinguished by a certain flavour which also defines their brand, such as Canadian Club and Chivas Regal. Whiskies such as the aforementioned, almost never identify one distillery in which the brand was made whereas one such blend found in Ireland is known to come from only one distillery – Jameson Whisky.

There is a distinct way in which Whiskies are produced which leads to a division in quality and popularity. One such distinction between these Whiskies is the cask strength of the Whisky itself. Cask Strength Whiskies which are also known as barrel proof are quite rare and are often the most expensive. Barrel proof Whisky is so named because it is bottled directly from the cask in its purest form. This allows the consumer to dilute the Whisky to their own preferred taste, if dilution is necessary at all. Single Cask Whisky, which is also known as Single barrel Whisky, is often bottled by specialists in the field. These Whiskies are bottled from a single barrel and are labelled from the individual cask from which it was bottled. Single Cask Whiskies are often labelled with a very specific amount of information identifying of the barrel itself as well as all associated numbers. Just because the brand of these Whiskies may be the same, the taste of the Whisky itself may differ from the casks used therefore the taste may not be consistent with a particular brand of Single Cask Whisky.

Contrary to belief, Whisky does not mature anywhere but in the cask. Therefore, the longer a Whisky sits bottled on a shelf, it is actually not getting better with age. The age of a whisky is only determined by the amount of time the Whisky has sat between distilling and bottling. What ages the Whisky is the time that is has been exposed to the cask itself which lends its efforts to the composition of the taste of the Whisky. Although a bottle that has been around for a long length of time and has been unopened is usually known to have a rarity value, it is not any "older" or better than Whiskies that could have been bottled recently from a cask of a similar wood and time than the "rare" Whisky. Whisky strengths average mostly around 40% alcohol by volume, as is the minimum mandate in certain countries, however the strength of Whisky can and does vary as it is known that Cask Strength Whisky contains almost as much as twice the alcohol percentage than that of their counterparts. Currently there are several nations that enjoy a healthy Whisky production, of which English, Canadian, Irish, Scotch, Welsh and American rank amongst the most popular.

English Whiskies have evolved and have again begun to be produced in great quantities. In late 2006, Norfolk became synonymous with Single Malt distilling as St. Georges Distillery produced the first English Single Malt in over a century. Historically it was the cities of Bristol and Liverpool that had gained fame as the centres of English Whisky production and distilling. Canadian Whiskies are known to have a light and smooth style about them. It is a law in the Dominion of Canada that each so named "Canadian" Whisky must be produced and aged in Canada as well as a base product of cereal grain be used before aging in wood barrels not larger than 700L. Such Whiskies may not be aged for less than three years to ensure the specific taste and quality expected of a Canadian Whisky. Though noted for their Rye Whiskies, Canada does not use this grain in their production, as Canadian Rye Whisky is actually derived from corn. Scotch Whiskies are known to be distilled several times, anywhere from two times up to 20+ times. Similar to Canadian regulations, Scotch must legally be aged for no less than three years in oak casks, markings on the bottle referencing its specific numbers as well as the age of the Whisky which serves as a guarantee, henceforth the Whisky has come to be known as Guaranteed Age Whisky. Scotch is mostly comprised of malt and grain variations which are mixed together to create certain blends. The most defining aspect of Scotch is that some of the distilleries treat their malt with peat smoke to give it a very distinct smoked flavour. Not all famous Scotch Whiskies use this in their Whisky production. Wales has again entered the fold of Whisky distillation. Operating the smallest distillery in the world, the Penderyn Distillery in 2000 was the first distillery to open since Whisky production ended in 1894. Penderyn Single Malt Whisky is exported across the globe since first becoming available to the public in 2004. Irish Whisky is historically known to use pot stills in the distilling process of this normally triple distilled spirit. Column stills are also used in Ireland to produce grain Whisky for blends, in which the most known types of Whisky from Ireland are Single Malt, Single Grain, Blended and Pure Pot Still Whiskies. Like their Canadian and Scottish counterparts, Irish Whiskies must be aged for no less than three years, however they are commonly aged three to four times more.

Imperial State Crown

Also known as Imperial Crown Martini

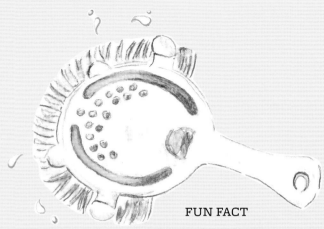

1 1/2 oz Whisky
1 oz Cointreau
1 oz Peach Schnapps
1/2 oz Raspberry Liqueur
1 oz cranberry juice
1 oz pineapple juice
a splash of Grenadine

In a shaker filled with ice, pour in all ingredients and shake and shimmy until frost appears on the shaker. Strain into a Martini glass and serve with a cherry and a slice of pineapple, peach, or raspberries!

FUN FACT

When Her Majesty tires of talking to someone during an official or informal visit, she spins her wedding ring or switches her ever-present handbag from one arm to the other.

QUOTE

"And what do you do?"

While knighting Premier League Chairman David Richards, November 2006

Queen Elizabeth II

1 oz ≈ 30 ml

Cross of St George

Also known as Old Fashioned

FUN FACTS

Unbeknownst to Palace officials, an undercover British tabloid reporter managed to get work at Buckingham Palace in 2003. He said that the Queen used Tupperware containers to house her cornflakes.

A lesser-known interest of Her Majesty is Scottish country dancing. Each year during her stay at Balmoral Castle, The Queen gives dances known as Gillies' Balls, for neighbours, estate and Castle staff and members of the local community.

1 sugar cube
2-3 dashes Bitters
2 orange slices
3 oz Whisky
1 oz Grenadine
Maraschino cherry for garnish

In a shaker, dissolve the sugar cube with whisky by shaking until the cube has vanished. Add in ice and other ingredients and resume shaking. This should help build your arm muscles! Strain into an old-fashioned glass over ice, drink and make another.

Queen's Flight

Also known as **Lawhill Cocktail**

2 oz rye Whisky
3/4 oz Sweet Vermouth
1 oz Absinthe
1/2 oz Grenadine
2 dashes Bitters

Stir (or shake vigorously for a fully-mixed and frothy cocktail) all ingredients in a shaker with ice, strain into a Martini glass (chips of ice should float in the drink), savour and enjoy.

FUN FACT

In 2007, Queen Elizabeth and His Royal Highness, Prince Philip celebrated their 60th wedding anniversary – the longest marriage of any British monarch.

QUOTE

"Have you been playing a long time?"

To four British guitar greats, Eric Clapton, Jimmy Page, Jeff Beck and Brian May, at reception for British music industry at Buckingham Palace March 2005

Queen Elizabeth II

1 oz ≈ 30 ml

Welsh Guards

Also known as Prince of Wales Cocktail

FUN FACTS

Only three Heads of State have celebrated Diamond Jubilees during the Queen's reign. King Bhumibol Adulyadej of Thailand celebrated in 2006; the former Sultan of Johor, now part of Malaysia, celebrated in 1955; and the late Emperor Hirohito of Japan celebrated in 1986.

Each morning, Her Majesty's breakfast table is laid out with porridge oats and cornflakes in Tupperware containers and yoghurt, along with light and dark marmalade.

1 1/2 oz Rye Whisky
1/4 tsp Maraschino
1 dash Bitters
1 tsp sugar
1 square of pineapple
1 oz chilled Champagne

In a mixing glass, add sugar and bitters and dissolve with a splash of water (or simple syrup). Continue to add Rye, Maraschino and pineapple chunk, then top off the glass with ice and shake hard in order to crush the pineapple. Strain into a chilled cocktail glass and top up with Champagne. Garnish with a lemon peel and enjoy!

Party at the Palace

Also known as Imperial Fizz cocktail

1 1/2 oz blended Whisky
1/2 oz Light Rum
juice of 1/2 a lemon
1 tsp powdered sugar

In a shaker, shake all ingredients (except carbonated water) with ice and strain into a highball glass over two-three ice cubes. Fill with carbonated water, stir, serve and enjoy this delightful experience.

FUN FACTS

The Queen's purses, mostly small black rectangles, are made for her by the royal purse maker.

The Queen's Christmas speech is written by the Queen and each has a strong religious framework which reflects current issues and often draws on her own experiences.

1 oz ≈ 30 ml

The Long Walk

FUN FACTS

The Queen and her troops have a very special relationship. She has been on the saluting base of her troops at every Trooping the Colour ceremony since becoming Queen. The only time she was not in front of her troops was in 1955, when a national rail strike forced the cancellation of the parade.

Queen Victoria was the last and only other British monarch to celebrate a Diamond Jubilee. Her Majesty will be the oldest monarch to celebrate a diamond jubilee at 86 years of age. Queen Victoria was 77 when she celebrated Diamond Jubilee in 1897.

2 oz Canadian Whisky
1 oz Sweet Vermouth
2 dashes Bitters
2 dashes Orange Curacao

In a shaker filled with ice, pour in all ingredients and shake until frost appears on the shaker. If you care to speed up the process, dance around with the shaker to your favourite song to pass the time to ensure ultimate frosting. Strain into a rocks glass filled with ice and serve. I can only suggest a long walk on a cold night after drinking several of these light cocktails.

The Maple Crown

2 oz Whisky
1/4–1/2 maple syrup
2 dashes Bitters
1/4–1/2 oz Grand Marnier
lemon twist garnish

In a mixing glass, pour ingredients over ice and shake twice.
Pour the mixture into a chilled Martini glass and serve with a
lemon twist. After a few of these semi-sweet refreshers, Canada
becomes closer to our hearts, and heads.

FUN FACTS

*The Queen was the first
British monarch to address
a joint session of Congress
in Washington, DC.*

*In 2010, Her Majesty, the
Queen delivered her
Christmas address from
Hampton Court Palace -
the first time this historic
building had been used.*

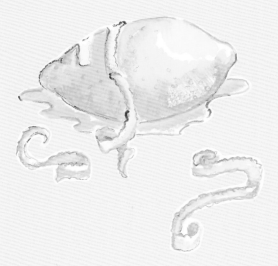

1 oz ≈ 30 ml

The Maple Leaf

1 oz Whisky
1/4 oz lemon juice
1 tsp maple syrup

Fill a shaker with ice and above-mentioned liqueurs, shake vigorously until hands are frozen (this creates a frothy head) strain into a whisky glass and enjoy a true, strong and northern recipe for refreshment.

A Jubilee Speech by Prime Minister David Cameron

On Wednesday 7, March 2012 in the House of Commons, London, The Prime Minister David Cameron delivered an address to the House of Commons praising Her Majesty, The Queen's contribution to her nations, in the year of the Diamond Jubilee.

Prime Minister Cameron said:

"On her first address to the nation as Queen, Her Majesty pledged that throughout all her life and with all her heart, she would strive to be worthy of the people's trust. This she has achieved beyond question. The nation holds her in its heart, not just as the figurehead of an institution but as an individual who has served this country with unerring grace, dignity and decency. The reign of Queen Elizabeth has been one of unparalleled change. From rationing through to the jet age, to the space age, to the digital age.

At her first investiture as Queen, the very first decoration she presented was a Victoria Cross for heroism in the Korean War. Since then, members of the Armed Forces – her Armed Forces – have been in action all over the world, from Aden to the Falklands, the Gulf, Iraq and Afghanistan. Around the world dictatorships have died and democracies have been born. And across the old British Empire, a vibrant Commonwealth of Nations has expanded and flourished. Throughout this extraordinary change, the longest-lived Monarch in our history has remained resolutely unchanged in her commitment and studious in her duties. It doesn't matter whether it is something we suspect she enjoys, like the Highland Games at Braemar or things we suspect she might be less keen on, like spending New Year's Eve in the Millennium Dome; she never, ever falters! She has always done her duty - and this stability is essential for our national life. While the sands of culture shift and the tides of politics ebb and flow, Her Majesty has been a permanent anchor; bracing Britain against the storms grounding us in certainty. And crucially, simultaneously, she has moved the Monarchy forward.

It has been said that "the art of progress is to preserve order amid change and change amid order" and in this the Queen is unparalleled. She has never shut the door on the future; instead she has led the way through it. Ushering in the television cameras; Opening up the Royal Collection and the Palaces; Hosting receptions and award ceremonies for every area of public life. It is easy now to take these things for granted - but we should remember that these were her initiatives. She was broadcasting to the nation every Christmas Day, thirty years before we let the cameras into this House. In doing these things she ended a thousand-year distance that existed between British monarchs and their people. Indeed, while much her life has been governed by tradition and protocol, the Queen has always taken a thoroughly pragmatic view of such matters.

On arriving at one engagement in Scotland, she noticed that the local Lord-Lieutenant was having considerable trouble extracting both himself and his sword from the official car in order to perform the introductions. While embarrassed civic dignitaries cleared their throats, the Queen cut straight through this seemingly insoluble ceremonial problem by walking up to the greeting line - hand outstretched - with the words "My Lord-Lieutenant appears to be having difficulty in getting out of the car so I'd better introduce myself, I'm the Queen." That human connection is a hallmark of her reign.

Over sixty years, according to one royal biographer, she has met four million people in person; that is equivalent to the entire population of New Zealand. In terms of garden parties alone, she has invited some two million people to tea. She is of course, Queen of sixteen countries and has surely travelled more widely than any other Head of State in history. As she herself has been heard to say – and it is a lesson perhaps for all of us in this House – 'I have to be seen to be believed.' All this has given her remarkable insight. Like her previous eleven Prime Ministers, I have been struck by Her Majesty's perspective on world events. And like my predecessors I am truly grateful for the way she handles our national interests. Last year's visit to Ireland was a lesson in statecraft. It showed once again that the

Queen can extend the hand of friendship like no other. She was the first monarch to visit China; the first to visit Russia; the first to pay a state visit to the Vatican. Her trip to post-apartheid South Africa was a statement that resounded across continents. And of course, there is the Commonwealth. It is doubtful whether this great alliance would ever have thrived without the dedication of Her Majesty. When the Queen became Head of the Commonwealth in 1952, it had eight members; today, it has 54.

No one has done more to promote this unique family of nations, spanning every continent, all the main religions and nearly a third of the world's population. And in all her realms, from Tuvalu to Barbados, from Papua New Guinea to St Vincent and the Grenadines, from Britain to Jamaica she is loved because she is a Queen for everyone; for each of us and for all of us. The Diamond Jubilee gives us the chance to show our gratitude. By the time she opens the Olympics, the Queen's Jubilee tour would have taken her and Prince Philip to every part of the United Kingdom. In June, London will see a huge pop concert, a great procession and the largest gathering on the Thames for more than three centuries – barges and cutters; narrow boats and motor boats; square riggers, naval vessels, the little ships of Dunkirk; all of them will be there to pay tribute to our magnificent Queen. Diamond is, I believe, the appropriate epithet for this Jubilee. For sixty years Her Majesty has been a point of light in our national life; brilliant, enduring and resilient. For that she has the respect of this House and the enduring affection of all her people."

Royal Scotch Drinks

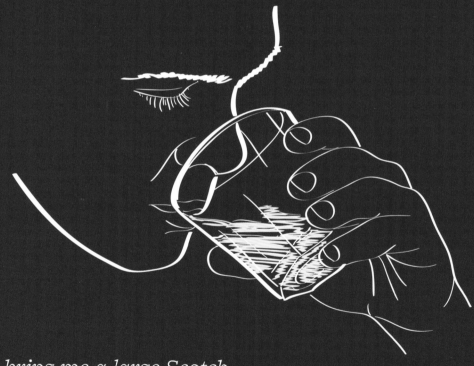

For God's sake bring me a large Scotch...

Reginald Maudling (1917-1979) British Politician

For the person who states that Whisky is Whisky, how acutely unaware they are of a finely distilled spirit. Out of all the Whiskies in the world, Scotch Whisky is by far one of the most notable, smooth and popular. There are only two basic types of Scotch from which all blends are made, Single Malt Scotch and Single Grain Scotch. Single Malt is made from only water and malted barley which is distilled in pot stills at one single distillery. Single Grain is produced at one single distillery but had other additives to its distilling process such as grains of other malted or unmalted cereals. Single Grain by definition does not mean that only one type of grain is used in production but that a single distillery is again the venue for its production though Single Grain Whisky is actually a mixture of grains which are used in the distilling process. Blended Scotch produced from Single Malt and Single Grain distilled at the same distillery are not to be confused and both classified as Single Grain, as there is a vast difference in their distillation process.

Though there are only a few types of Scotch, there are actually more blends that are made and defined by the term 'Scotch'. Blended Malt Scotch Whisky means a blend of two or more Single Malt Scotch Whiskies from different distilleries. Blended Grain Scotch is comprised of two or more Single Grain Scotches from different distilleries not just one single distillery. Blended Scotch is a blend of one or more Single Malt Scotches with one or more Single Grain Scotches. The types of Scotch are mutually exclusive in that they are so structured by distinctive categories. Knowing that Scotch is subject to a very stringent set of rules set for it to be termed Scotch, new regulations set forth in 2009 changed the formal definition of Scotch in a way that reflected both the traditional and current practice of distilling. Before the regulation changes (SWR) in 2009, any combination of Scotch qualified as Blended Scotch. This also included Single Malt Scotch.

Similar to the Scotch Whisky Act of 1988, SWR 2009 (provision 5) states that the only whisky that is allowed to be produced in Scotland is Scotch. In defining the term 'made' or 'manufactured' (as per the official term), the regulations state that manufacturing is "keeping for the purpose of maturation; and keeping, or using, for the purpose of blending, except for domestic blending for domestic consumption". By regulating to this extreme, this regulation prevents the existence of two grades of Scotch that would be a derivative of Scotland, Scotch Whisky and Whisky defined as a product of Scotland. The Scotch Whisky Association continues to protect the production of 'Scotch' by passing regulations that make it difficult for other Whiskies that would be made in Scotland to be a distinctive product of Scotland, much like Scotch. Regulations passed prohibit any Whisky production in Scotland that is not defined as Scotch as well as prohibiting the blending and maturing of Whisky in Scotland that does not adhere to the distilling process set forth by the Association. The Scotch Whisky Association continues to help Scotch remain a distinct product of Scotland without imitations capitalising on the hard work and history of true Scotch Whisky.

90% of the Scotch (Whisky) produced in Scotland is a blend which contains both Malt and Grain Whisky. Famous Scotch producers such as Ballantines, Chivas Regal, Cutty Sark, Dewars, J&B, Johnnie Walker and The Famous Grouse, all combine various malt and grain Whiskies in the production of their individual and distinctive style and brand.

Britannia

Also known as Aberdeen Angus Cocktail

2 oz Scotch
1 oz Drambuie Liqueur
1 tbsp honey
2 tbsp lime juice

In a mixing glass, combine all ingredients and shake until honey is fluid. Pour into a rocks glass filled with ice and garnish with a lemon twist.

1 oz ≈ 30 ml

Balmoral Castle

Also known as Highland Fling Cocktail

FUN FACTS

Since 1952, The Queen has undertaken approximately 112 State visits accompanied by The Duke of Edinburgh, the last being to the Republic of Ireland in 2010 in which she is the first reigning British Monarch to visit since Ireland gained independence in the 1920's.

In 1992, The Queen issued a writ against The Sun newspaper after it published the full text of her Christmas broadcast two days before transmission. She later accepted an apology and a £200,000 donation to charity.

1 1/2 oz Scotch
1 oz Sweet Vermouth
dashes of Orange Bitters
green olive

Stir (or shake vigorously for a fully mixed and frothy cocktail) all ingredients in a shaker with ice, strain into a Martini glass, garnish with olive, savour and enjoy.

Birkhall Blend

Also known as Tilt the Kilt Cocktail

1 1/2 oz Scotch
1/2 oz Triple Sec
1 oz orange juice

In a shaker half-filled with ice, combine all of the ingredients and shake well – that's right...until frosty cold. Strain into an old-fashioned glass half-filled with ice cubes and garnish with an orange slice. Enjoy this alternative way to consuming vitamin C.

FUN FACTS

The Queen has given out approximately 80,000 Christmas puddings to staff continuing the custom of King George V and King George VI. In addition, The Queen gives all her staff a gift at Christmas time.

When the Queen was a young girl, she received tuition from her father, as well as sessions with Henry Marten, the Vice-Provost of Eton. She was also instructed in religion by the Archbishop of Canterbury.

1 oz ≈ 30 ml

Palace of Holyroodhouse

Also known as Bonny Doon Cocktail

FUN FACTS

The Queen learned to drive in 1945 when she joined the Army.

Since 1952, the Queen has given royal assent to more than 3500 Acts of Parliament.

1 1/2 oz Scotch
1/2 oz Sweet Vermouth
2 tsp Benedictine
2 tsp Grenadine

Stir (or shake vigorously for a fully mixed and frothy cocktail) all ingredients in a shaker with ice, strain into a rocks glass filled with ice, or to smarten up – make sure the shaker is frosty and strain into a Martini glass, garnish with a cherry, savour, enjoy and make another.

Royal Standard

Also known as Prince Edward Cocktail

1 3/4 oz Scotch
1/2 oz Lillet Blanc
1/4 oz Drambuie
add orange slice

In a rocks glass half-filled with ice, add all ingredients and stir until your fingers are sore. Strain into a small snifter and garnish with an orange slice. Perfection in a glass!

1 oz ≈ 30 ml

Scots Guard

Also known as Commodore Cocktail

1 tsp powdered sugar
1/2 lemon
2 dashes Bitters
1 oz Scotch
1 oz Sweet Vermouth
Ginger Ale

In a mixing glass, add all ingredients with the exception of the ginger ale and give it a few good strong shakes. Pour into a rocks glass filled with ice and top off with ginger ale. Repeat these steps until your vision becomes blurry.

Order of the Thistle

Also known as Loch Lomond Cocktail #2

1 oz Scotch
1/2 oz Peach Schnapps
1 oz Blue Curacao
3 oz grapefruit juice
1/2 oz lemon juice

Stir (or shake vigorously for a fully mixed and frothy cocktail) all ingredients in a shaker with ice, strain into a Martini glass rimmed with flavoured sugar crystals, serve with a lemon twist and savour the flavour.

FUN FACT

Every year The Queen sends Christmas trees to Westminster Abbey, Wellington Barracks, St Paul's Cathedral; St Giles, Edinburgh; The Canongate Kirk, Edinburgh; Crathie Church and local schools and churches in the Sandringham area.

QUOTE

"Like all the best families we have our share of eccentricities, of impetuous and wayward youngsters and of family disagreements."

Queen Elizabeth II

1 oz ≈ 30 ml

The Royal Mile

Also known as Caleigh Cocktail

1 1/2 oz Scotch
1/2 oz Blue Curacao
1/2 oz white Crème De Cocoa
1/2 oz white Chocolate Liqueur

In a mixing glass filled with ice, pour ingredients over ice and shake two-three times. Pour the mixture into a chilled Martini glass and serve with white chocolate shavings. Highly recommended for those with a sweet tooth.

79

St Andrews Elixir

1 1/2 oz Scotch
1/2 oz Sweet Vermouth
1/2 oz Dry Vermouth
2 dashes Bitters

In a mixing glass filled with ice, shake long and hard and immediately strain into a cocktail glass filled with ice cubes. Enjoy – it's that simple!

Address to HM The Queen, by the Lord Speaker

Westminster Hall, Tuesday 20 March 2012

'Most Gracious Sovereign,

We, the Lords Spiritual and Temporal, are assembled here today to celebrate sixty years of Your reign. We record with warmth and affection our appreciation of Your dedicated service to Your people, and Your unequalled sense of public duty over the years – service and duty to which You have only recently, and so movingly, re-dedicated Yourself.

We celebrate too Your stewardship of Your high office. You have personified continuity and stability while ensuring that Your role has evolved imperceptibly, with the result that the Monarchy is as integral a part of our national life today as it was 60 years ago.

We rejoice in this Jubilee and we give thanks for all that it represents. At the same time, we record our gratitude for the support which You have received throughout Your reign from His Royal Highness Prince Philip, for in this year of jubilee we celebrate his service too.

This is one of the first of many celebrations to be held up and down the land. In the coming months You and the Duke will travel widely throughout the Kingdom. But today You have come to Parliament, the constitutional heart of the nation, and granted us the privilege of being the first of Your people formally to honour Your Jubilee. And where better to begin the celebrations than here, in the splendour of Westminster Hall – a hall of kings and queens for almost a millennium.

While this Hall has seen many historic events, few are permanently commemorated. So we look forward with great anticipation to the unveiling of the stained glass window which members of both Houses have commissioned in honour of this day. When placed in the window above the great doors, Your Coat of Arms and Royal Cypher will bathe the Hall in colour and be seen daily by members and staff as they walk through to their offices -and by the many thousands of visitors we receive here weekly, from both home and abroad.

For we must remember that Your Jubilee will be celebrated with joy in Your other realms and territories, and throughout the rest of the Commonwealth. The Commonwealth as we know it today is of course one of the great achievements of Your reign and under Your leadership continues to flourish, with a membership of 54 countries. It is still growing. It is a tremendous force for good in the world and we are aware of its special personal significance to You.

Many of us present here today take an active part in the work of the United Kingdom Branch of the Commonwealth Parliamentary Association. We work to share our experiences, to learn from one another, and to promote democracy. But our efforts are as nothing compared with those of Your Majesty in the service of Your beloved Commonwealth. Over the years You have visited all but two Commonwealth countries - some, many times - and attended all Heads of Government meetings since 1997. We look on with admiration and pride at the triumphs of some of Your recent tours and it is significant that members of the Royal Family are representing You this year at the Jubilee celebrations being held in all those lands in which You are Head of State.

Your Majesty, the Lords Spiritual and Temporal in Parliament Assembled give thanks for this Your Diamond Jubilee. We look forward to the years to come and we pray that You and Your realms may enjoy the peace, plenty and prosperity that have so distinguished Your reign.'

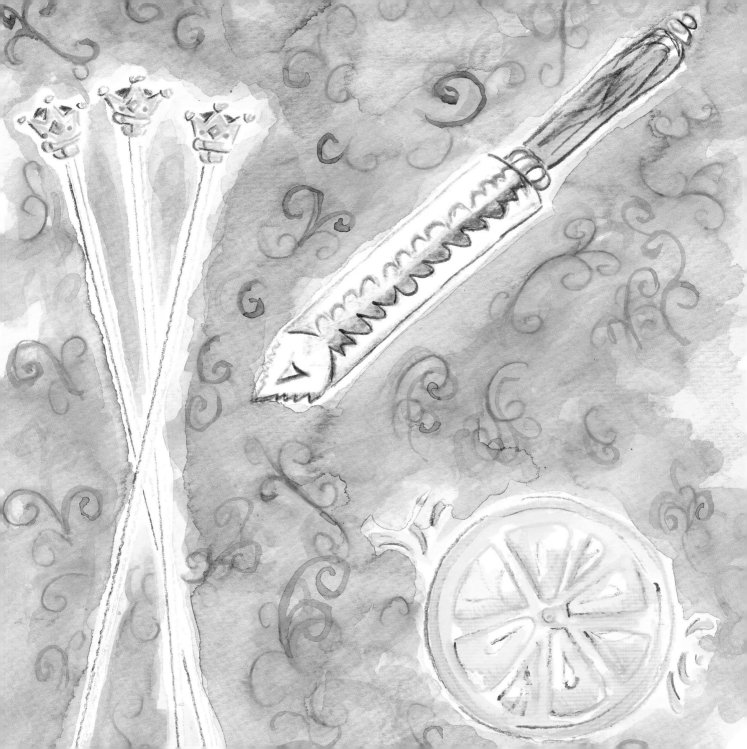

Royal Rum Drinks

There's nought no doubt so much the spirit calms as Rum and true religion.

Lord Byron (1788-1824), English Poet

Like a child to a sweet shop, so are adults to Rum – Yum! Sugar is sweet and sweet comes from sugar, much like Rum and cane spirit which are both born from the same element. Both of these smooth and delicious spirits are made simply by distilling water together with fermented sugar which is from pure sugar cane. Most of the world's Rums are the product of molasses which is the by-product of boiling sugar cane and extracting the crystallised sugar. Molasses is also used for more than distilling alcohol. It was the colonial sugar-mill operators who have been credited with the discovery of molasses, as they noticed that when sugar was mixed with water and left out on its own in the sun the mixture would ferment. It was during the 1650s that this newly-found product was used to distil alcohol. In our Caribbean colonies Rum was known as 'Kill Devil' (as it was known to give those who imbibed too much, intense hangovers), or 'Rumbullion' which was shortened to the term we know now.

In our colonies where Rum was produced it was often referred to as a medicine to cure all that ails the body. It was mainly used to treat aches and pains for those living on the islands and throughout the tropics. Rum was inexpensive to manufacture and took little to no time in the grand scheme of things which allowed the sugar plantation owners to sell it at a heavily discounted price. By selling such a commodity to naval ships, sugar plantation owners were able to attract naval ships to the area, which would make frequent visits to purchase the alcohol. These visits would help discourage pirates that would often prey on the wealthy sugar plantations. It was not long before the British navy (in the 1730s) adopted a daily ration of a half-pint of 160-proof Rum. This ration of pure distilled Rum was further modified by mixing it half and half with water to produce a distinct drink called 'Grog'. This maritime concoction continued to remain a staple of the British Royal Navy until 1969. As Rum was sold to Navy ships and their sailors, it was not long before this alcohol was presented to the world beyond the Caribbean. By the turn of the 18th century, Rum was a commodity that formed a new export for trade.

The British island colonies in the Caribbean produced and shipped Rum home to not only Great Britain but to our other colonies such as North America. Rum became so popular and it was during this time that it was made into punches and other related drinks which overtook Gin in popularity. The exporting of Rum to our North American colonies (eventually the United States and Canada) in exchange for lumber and dried cod from New England eventually gave way to the export of raw molasses to newly-founded distilleries in North America which helped avoid British taxes and laws which were implemented by Parliament. It was illegal at this time to trade spirits directly between the colonies, as doing so would prove damaging to British distillers. However, this law did not stop the illegal smuggling of Rum. To this day, the trade of Rum is very much alive and well, as Canada's 300-year-old tradition of trading Rum for dried cod fish continues in the maritime provinces. The peoples of Nova Scotia and Newfoundland trade their goods in favour of importing golden Rums from Antigua, Barbados and Jamaica. Europe today, is primarily a blender of imported Rums, where both Britain and France continue to import Rums from the former Caribbean colonies for aging, bottling and selling.

The product of Molasses consists of over fifty percent sugar and is high in other elements and minerals that help contribute to the flavour of Rum. There are several varieties and types of Rum, but one must know that the choice of stills does have a significant effect on the final product. As Rum is distilled, it is naturally a clear translucent spirit. It is the addition of caramel colouring and the length of barrel aging that gives it its heavy or light appearance. As Rum is a natural product, so is the colouring that is used, as caramel colouring is but burnt sugar. Heavy Rum and light Rum are distinguished by the distilling processes used in their manufacturing. Lighter Rums are purified and blended several times whilst being produced in column stills. Light Rums are so named as they are 'charcoal filtered' and aged in oak casks which add to a smooth flow on the palate. Many of the world's light Rums have little flavour or smell which closely resemble another clear alcohol – Vodka.

Heavier Rums differ from their lighter counterparts in that they are distilled in pot stills. This form of distilling heavy Rums is very similar to the processes used to produce Cognacs and Scotch, due to the fact that the pot stills are less "efficient" than column stills. Due in part to this difference it is the extra-naturally produced additives such as fusel oils and flavours that add to the overall flavour of the Rum. Like other alcohols, several brands of Rum are produced by blending both light (column distilled) and heavy (pot distilled) Rums to create a specific flavour and brand. Rums made from cane juice, such as those from the island nations of Haiti and Martinique have a naturally smooth palate due in part to the distilling process in which the particular cane juice is fermented with airborne wild yeast or a cultured yeast for specific amounts of time. Light rums are aged for as little as one day and up to several weeks to create a full and heavy Rum. Rum can be broken down into several classifications which are: Añejo, Dark, Gold, Light, Spiced and Flavoured.

Añejo Rum refers to age-dated Rums which are from different batches which are blended together to create a distinct flavour of a brand from year to year. These Rums will often be labelled with the age of the youngest rum used to mix the particular blend, whereas a handful of French-producing islands label their bottles with the date of vintage. Dark Rum lends its name to the certain colour of the Rum, such as Brown Rum, Black Rum and Red Rum. This class of Rum is darker than Gold Rum as it is aged longer in their charred oak barrels. Dark Rums have a much stronger flavour than their lighter counterparts, as they have a distinct trace of spices with a heavy flavour of molasses and caramel colour. Dark Rum is heavy-bodied and is most commonly used for drinking straight up as well as for use in mixed drinks and cooking. It is mainly produced on the island nations of Jamaica, Haiti and Martinique although two of the most popular and award-winning dark Rums are products of Central America and not the Caribbean. These two nations, Nicaragua and Guatemala produced the award-winning Flor de Cana and Ron Zacapa Centenario. Golden Rums are commonly referred to as Amber Rum which are darker that light Rums in colour but not as dark as fully-fledged dark Rum. Golden Rums are found to be medium-bodied and are aged for several years in their oak casks which enhances their smoothness on the palate. Golden Rums are normally aged in charred white oak barrels which are usually the by-product from the aging of Bourbon (Whisky). These Rums have more of a distinct flavour to them and are stronger that Silver Rums, but not as strong as their darker counterparts.

Light or White Rums are generally of a light-bodied composition. Usually clear in colour they are known to have very little flavour. When light Rums are aged in casks, the Rum is then usually filtered to remove any impurity such as colour. This process helps create a distinct palate which is extremely smooth. White Rums are used mostly as mixers which are known to blend well with fruit flavours. Many Rum Punches are created and served with fruit juices that are very popular in resort areas of the Caribbean. Spiced Rums are known to be dark in colour and use the same base and process as its gold Rum cousin. The spiced flavour of these Rums are due to the addition of spices such as Aniseed, Cinnamon, Rosemary and Pepper as well as the caramel colour that is used in the distilling process. Some spiced Rums are quite dark whereas cheaper varieties of this spiced favourite are based from white Rum which has been darkened by artificial means. Flavoured Rums are fairly new to the alcohol market as a handful of manufacturers have started infusing their Rum with hints of fruit flavours. This variety of Rum is usually less than 40% alcohol and is used to enhance mixed drinks or to sip cold over ice as a light refresher on hot days. The most popular flavoured Rums on the market today are Orange, Coconut, Lime, Banana and Mango. Rum is not to be misunderstood as a cheap and lessened version of its other alcohol-based cousins.

As with other sipping spirits such as Cognac and Scotch, Rum too has a distinct market and demand for its premium and super-premium blends. Such Rums are produced and aged with the utmost of care. They have a bolder body and stronger flavour than other Rums and are produced to be drunk in their virgin form. Like premium Rum, over-proof Rum is distinctive in the Rum family. This type of Rum has a much higher content than the standard 40% rating. In fact, most over-proof Rums consist of levels which are in excess of 60% alcohol and have even been produced in the range of 75-80% alcohol which is not uncommon in this finely-distilled sugary sweet liquid candy.

Duke of Normandy

Also known as Sir Walter Raleigh Cocktail

1 tbsp Grenadine
1 tsp Orange Curacao
1 tsp lemon juice
1/2 Rum
1/4 Brandy

In a shaker half-filled with ice, add all ingredients and again put on your winter gloves. Shake vigorously until frost appears on the outside of the shaker. Strain into a cocktail glass and serve with an orange twist.

With the birth of Prince Andrew at Buckingham Palace in 1960, Her Majesty became the first reigning Sovereign to have a child since Queen Victoria, who had her youngest child, Princess Beatrice, in 1857.

The Queen hosted the first women-only event "Women of Achievement" at Buckingham Palace in March, 2004.

1 oz ≈ 30 ml

Sandringham

Also known as Queens Park Sizzle Cocktail

FUN FACT

In 1969 the first television film about the ordinary family life of the Queen and the Royal Family was made. It aired on the eve of the Investiture of Prince Charles as Prince of Wales.

QUOTE

"I have to be seen to be believed."

Queen Elizabeth II

3 oz Demerara Rum
3/4 oz lime juice
1/2 oz Simple Syrup
3 heavy dashes Bitters
fresh mint

In a tall glass filled with crushed ice, add the above contents including the leftover lime from which the juice was squeezed. Top off the glass with more crushed ice and using your favourite swizzle stick, swizzle until the glass is frosty cold. Serve with mint leaves and a large straw for easy drinking.

Prom at the Palace

Also known as **Saxon Cocktail**

1 3/4 oz Light Rum
1/2 tsp Grenadine syrup
1/2 juice of a fresh squeezed lime
1 twist orange peel

In a mixing glass filled with ice combine the rum, Grenadine and lime juice, then swizzle until the mixture is equally distributed. Garnish with an orange peel and enjoy the evening!

1 oz ≈ 30 ml

Caribbean Queen

Also known as Pelican Punch Cocktail

1 1/2 oz Raspberry Rum
1/2 oz Dark Rum
1/4 oz 151 proof Rum
1 1/2 oz pineapple juice
1 1/2 oz orange juice
1 oz Sweet & Sour Mix

In a Hurricane glass filled with ice, mix all ingredients and stir until well-blended. Serve as is with an orange slice or a lemon wheel. For an added kick, add a floater of Rum to the top of the drink (simply add a shot of Rum on top of the drink and do not mix). Enjoy!

Royal Mustique

Also known as Bahama Mama Cocktail

1/4 oz Coffee Liqueur
1/2 oz Dark Rum
1/2 oz Coconut Liqueur
1/4 oz 151 proof (high proof) Rum
juice of 1/2 lemon
4 oz pineapple juice
strawberry or cherry for garnish

In a mixing glass filled with cubed ice, add all ingredients and shake until frothy cold. Pour into a Collins glass filled with cracked ice and garnish with a cherry and/or strawberry for added colour and flavour. This wonderful cocktail will transport you to the white sandy beaches of the Caribbean, if you have more than just a couple!

FUN FACTS

The first 'Royal walkabout' took place during a visit by The Queen and The Duke of Edinburgh to Australia and New Zealand in 1970. The practice was introduced to allow them to meet a greater number of people which included the public, not simply officials and dignitaries.

Queen Elizabeth II loves to travel. She can be seen today at the age of 85 travelling in a domestic and international capacity. Her Majesty has travelled to 129 different countries on 256 official overseas visits. She has also travelled in a private capacity visiting her late sister, Princess Margaret, at her home in Mustique three times, as well as choosing Canada as her dominion of preference, visiting it over 30 times during her reign.

1 oz ≈ 30 ml

Montserrat Majesty

Also known as Hurricane Cocktail

FUN FACTS

The Queen has sat for approximately 140 official portraits during her lifetime, two of which were with The Duke of Edinburgh. Her Majesty was just seven years old when she sat for her first portrait in 1933, which was commissioned by her mother and painted by the Hungarian artist Philip Alexius de László.

In 1942, Her Majesty (as Princess Elizabeth) was appointed Colonel-In-Chief of the Grenadier Guards on her 16th Birthday and visited the regiment to personally inspect them. This was her first solo public engagement. She spent the day with the Grenadier Tank Battalion in Southern Command in what was to be the first in a series of public engage-ments that would eventually span the rest of her life.

2 oz Light Rum
2 oz Dark Rum
2 oz passion fruit juice
1 oz orange juice
juice of 1/2 lime
1 tbsp Simple Syrup
1 tbsp Grenadine

In a large shaker, squeeze the juice from the lime over ice and continue to add the rest of the ingredients. Shake long and hard until the mixture is of a frothy cold consistency (you should be a pro at this by now) and strain into a Hurricane glass which will be garnished with an orange slice and a cherry which complete this tropical refresher.

St Lucia's Lilibet

Also known as Bahamas Rum Punch

1oz Rum
1/2 oz Coconut Rum
pineapple juice
orange juice
a splash of Campari

This recipe is simple and quick. Simply pour equal parts orange and pineapple juices into a large glass filled with ice, add in the Rum and colour it red with Campari. Swizzle until the mixture is even in colour. Sit back and enjoy this delightful, light and refreshing cocktail.

FUN FACTS

An important innovation during The Queen's reign was the 1962 opening of the Queen's Gallery at Buckingham Palace to display items from the Royal Collection. Established by The Duke of Edinburgh, the new Queen's Gallery occupied the space of the Palace's bomb-damaged private chapel.

The Queen who allows Parliament to convene in the Royal Palace of Westminster (Houses of Parliament) is not allowed to enter the House of Commons due in fact because she is not a member.

1 oz ≈ 30 ml

Jamaican Queen

Also known as Mojito Highball

FUN FACT

*The first football match
The Queen attended was
the 1953 FA Cup Final.*

QUOTE

*"I cannot lead you into battle.
I do not give you laws or
administer justice but I
can do something else – I
can give my heart and my
devotion to these old islands
and to all the peoples of our
brotherhood of nations."*

Queen Elizabeth II

2 oz Rum
1 tsp sugar
1/2 lime
Soda Water

In a highball glass, mix all ingredients together and swizzle until sugar dissolves. Add ice and top off with soda water. Simply garnish with a lime slice and enjoy the company you are with, be it with a group of friends or your new friend, the Mojito Highball.

Address to HM The Queen, by Speaker of the House of Commons

Westminster Hall, Tuesday 20 March 2012

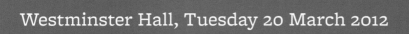

Most Gracious Sovereign,

We, Your faithful Commons are honoured to be here to commemorate and celebrate the sixty years of Your reign. We too are pleased to have contributed to the Jubilee Window to be revealed shortly and which will mark this occasion permanently. Time is better preserved in this historic place than in fallible human memory.

Time also tells its own story. Sixty years ago, rationing meant rather more than a short wait before the arrival of the latest electronic item. Sixty years ago, Britain had just emerged from a war of an intensity never seen before or since and had slipped into the shadow of the Korean conflict. Sixty years ago, a new "Elizabethan Era" was awaited with enthusiasm tinged with uncertainty about the challenges ahead for the country.

If, as Gandhi asserted, "The best way to find yourself is to lose yourself in the service of others", then Your Majesty must have found Yourself countless times over the past six decades. You have dedicated Your life to others. The daily example that You set, mirrored by our courageous armed forces of which You are Commander-in-Chief, is extraordinary. Yet perhaps Your Majesty's most profound contribution has been to the continuity that has made change manageable.

For transformation is inevitably turbulent. It has been Your singular accomplishment, Your unique capacity, to hold together that which could have been torn asunder. You have moved with the times and allowed the times to move around the rest of society.

This is a different Britain from 1952 but not one detached from then. We are in so many ways a much bigger, brighter and better United Kingdom. This is a land where men and women today are equal under the law and where Your people are respected, regardless of how they live, how they look or how they love. This is a nation of many races, faiths and customs, now beginning to be reflected in Parliament. All this progress has occurred during Your reign. You have become, to many of us, a kaleidoscope Queen of a kaleidoscope country in a kaleidoscope Commonwealth.

Royal Brandy Drinks

When I am an old woman, I shall wear purple, With a red hat which doesn't go and doesn't suit me, And I shall spend my pension on Brandy and summer gloves and satin sandals, and say we've no money for butter.

Jenny Joseph (1932–present) British Poet

Brandy or "Burnt Wine" is a derivative of the Dutch "brandewijn" which is an alcohol (spirit) produced from the distillation of wine. Unlike its grain counterparts Gin and Whisky, which can be made throughout the year, Brandy is an alcohol that is dependent on the seasons. The ripened fruits that are harvested must first be produced into wine, which is then distilled for the production of the alcohol from which Brandy is made. In addition to fermented grapes, Brandy is also produced from other fermented fruits which are referred to in French as 'eaux-de-vie'. Due in part to the ingredients used, Brandy is an agricultural alcohol where its base must be ripened in order to enter the fermenting and distilling process, much like Rum. Brandy can vary in alcohol content, but usually measures about 35%-60% alcohol by volume.

Brandy's origination corresponds with the growth and development of the process of distillation. Today's Brandy can trace its roots to the 12th century eventually becoming widely popularised by the 14th century. To make its transport easier for merchants, wine was initially distilled as a preservation method for long journeys as well as a way to lessen its tariffs which were excised by its mass. Upon arrival of the wine, the intent was to replace the water that was removed before consumption. After travelling for vast amounts of time in storage casks made of wood, it was found that "Brandy" was an improvement over the original spirit being transported. Mostly known as an after-dinner drink, it was common that during the turn of the 20th century through to the 1960s prominent gentlemen in society when gathered, would excuse themselves to enjoy a Brandy and a smoke. Brandies are typically aged like its other alcoholic counterparts in wooden casks, whilst some others are coloured with caramel colouring. There are certain labels that use both aging and colouring to produce their Brandy, whilst other labels use fruit flavouring to create a distinct flavour and brand. As an agricultural alcohol whose base is primarily comprised of grapes, it is not unexpected that most brandies originate from regions of high wine production. Some of the best Brandies (at present, as well as historically) happen to come from regions that produce the best wines such as France, Spain and the far reaches of Eastern Europe, as well as the Eurasian plateau (where Brandy was referred to as Cognac). Different types of Brandies have often tended to be specific to their location of production therefore this identifying trait leads to certain Brandy-making areas specifying the type of grape or fruit that can be used and where it can be grown.

Historically it has been the vast cellars of the Romanov Court in Russia's Imperial Capital of St. Petersburg that have been famed for their expansive and quality cognacs, Brandies and wines. This collection became legendary as much of it was lost after the collapse of the Romanov dynasty. The October Revolution of 1917, saw the grand Winter Palace stormed and once the Palace was taken, the army took a week-long hiatus so that they could imbibe large quantities of the collection whilst they pillaged the Palace for its treasures, art and fine furnishings. Though the Russian monarchy ended and its famed collection of wines, Brandies and Cognacs made legend by communist thugs and murders, the age of Russian Brandy production was anything but dead. As Russia began to emerge from its dark days of the revolution and head into the Soviet era, it was the Communist governments of the day that kept the production of Brandy a source of pride for the people. The Soviet Union produced some of the best quality brandies which are still sought after today, especially their famous jubilee Brandies of 1967, 1977 and 1987.

Brandy, for the connoisseur, is mostly drank neat or on the rocks but others may choose to mix it with additional liqueurs or mixers to create other cocktails, such as the well-known Brandy Alexander, Brandy Old Fashioned, Brandy Sour or the Sidecar. For those who choose to enjoy Brandy in its pure form, they would know that when Brandy is consumed at room temperature, it is usually cupped in the palm of the hand (in a special glass known as a 'Brandy Snifter') which slightly warms it. Some people choose to heat their Brandies before consuming it, however, excessive heating of the spirit may cause the alcohol vapours to become too strong thus rendering the Brandy overpowering. Contrary to popular belief, Brandy fares better at a lower temperature which would mean that the spirit should be consumed cooled rather than heated to fully enjoy the full and smooth feel of the alcohol. Heating the Brandy tends to make the alcohol thinner and less full-bodied which can create a burning sensation when consumed.

The Throne

Also known as Brandy Swizzle

1 1/2 oz lime juice
1 tsp superfine sugar
2 oz Brandy
1 dash Bitters
3 oz Club Soda
crushed ice

It has been a while, but let me reintroduce you to our friend the shaker. In the shaker add the lime juice, sugar, Brandy and Bitters then continue to shake and shimmy vigorously to your favourite tunes until your hands hurt from the cold. Then, in a Collins glass filled with crushed ice, swizzle the ice until the glass itself is frosty cold. Once the desired frost has appeared, strain the contents of the strainer into the glass and top off with club soda. Garnish with a lime rind and withdraw to the garden.

Royal Coat of Arms

Also known as Duke of Cornwall

FUN FACT

The Queen's first Commonwealth tour began on 24 November 1953. The tour included visits to Bermuda, Jamaica, Panama, Fiji, Tonga, New Zealand, Australia, the Cocos Islands, Ceylon, Aden, Uganda, Libya, Malta and Gibraltar. The total distance covered was 43,618 miles.

QUOTE

"It is easy enough to define what the Commonwealth is not. Indeed this is quite a popular pastime."

Queen Elizabeth II

1 oz Apple Brandy
1 oz Sweet Sherry
2 oz sparkling apple juice

In an old-fashioned glass, stir in all ingredients with broken ice, give a quick swirl of the glass and serve. You know what they say, an apple a day...

Royal Cypher

Also known as Brandy Julep

2 1/2 oz Brandy
1 tsp powdered sugar
5 mint leaves

In an empty Collins glass, place at the bottom of the glass the sugar, mint leaves and Brandy. Follow through with filling the glass with finely-shaved ice and stir ever so gently so that the mint leaves rise to the top. You must be gentle with this process so as not to bruise the mint leaves. You may garnish with a pineapple, orange, lemon and/or a cherry, however I prefer less fruit and more drink.

FUN FACTS

Her Majesty was the first British Monarch to visit China when she visited in 1986.

Her Majesty was the first Monarch to send her children to boarding school, to escape the ever- present media intrusion into their lives.

1 oz ≈ 30 ml

Royal Peculiar

Also known as Brandy Punch

FUN FACTS

In 1953, The Queen made the first Christmas Broadcast from overseas (rather than from the UK) broadcasting live from New Zealand. The first televised broadcast was aired live in 1957. The first pre-recorded broadcast took place in 1960 to allow transmission around the world.

Her Majesty has 30 God-children.

2 oz Brandy
1/2 oz Triple Sec
2 1/2 oz Dry Ginger Ale

Combine all the ingredients in a rocks glass filled with crushed ice. Dip a quick swizzle and garnish with mint leaves and a fruit slice of your choice if so desired.

Royal Mews

Also known as Horses Neck Cocktail

2 oz Brandy
5 oz Ginger Ale
2 dashes Bitters
1 lemon spiral

In a highball glass filled with ice, pour the Brandy, Ginger Ale and Bitters into the glass and swizzle well. The lemon spiral should be draped over the rim of the glass for proper presentation, but I tend to put mine on a friend's glass so that it does not obstruct my imbibing ability of this light and tasty cocktail. Enjoy!

FUN FACT

The Queen has made an annual Christmas Broadcast to the Commonwealth every year of her reign except in 1969, when a repeat of the film 'Royal Family' was shown and a written message from The Queen issued.

QUOTE

"The upward course of a nation's history is due, in the long run, to the soundness of heart of its average men and women."

Queen Elizabeth II

1 oz ≈ 30 ml

A Right Royal

Also known as Brandy Cocktail

FUN FACT

The Queen undertook her first State Visit as Princess Elizabeth, with King George VI and Queen Elizabeth to South Africa from February to May 1947. The tour included Rhodesia and Bechuanaland, Swaziland and Basutoland (now Lesotho). The Princess celebrated her 21st birthday in Cape Town, South Africa where she made a speech dedicating her life in service to the people of the Commonwealth.

QUOTE

"I myself prefer my New Zealand eggs for breakfast."

Queen Elizabeth II

2 oz Brandy
1/4 tsp sugar syrup
2 dashes Bitters
1 twist lemon peel

In a mixing glass shake all ingredients well with ice until a light foam appears. Strain into a cocktail glass and garnish with a lemon peel. You may choose to serve to others, but I sometimes find that when I have more, the merrier everyone else is!

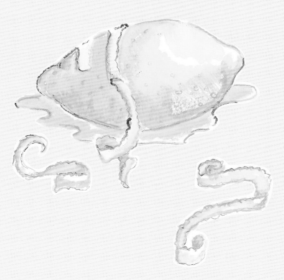

Summer Solstice Smash

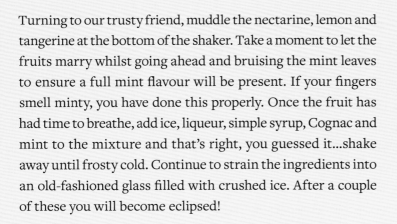

1/2 yellow nectarine
1 lemon wedge
1 tangerine wedge
4 chocolate mint leaves
1/2 oz Peach Liqueur
1 oz Cognac
1/2 oz Simple Syrup

Turning to our trusty friend, muddle the nectarine, lemon and tangerine at the bottom of the shaker. Take a moment to let the fruits marry whilst going ahead and bruising the mint leaves to ensure a full mint flavour will be present. If your fingers smell minty, you have done this properly. Once the fruit has had time to breathe, add ice, liqueur, simple syrup, Cognac and mint to the mixture and that's right, you guessed it...shake away until frosty cold. Continue to strain the ingredients into an old-fashioned glass filled with crushed ice. After a couple of these you will become eclipsed!

FUN FACT

In 1969, Her Majesty sent a message of congratulations to the Apollo 11 astronauts for the first moon landing on the 21st July, 1969. The message was microfilmed and deposited on the moon in a metal container.

QUOTE

"They are not royal. They just happen to have me as their aunt."

Queen Elizabeth II

Brighton Punch

FUN FACTS

Her Majesty's first State Visit as Queen was technically to Kenya, as King George VI died when she was there on tour. She ascended the throne at Tree Top Villas where she took the name Elizabeth II as Queen.

The Queen has nine Royal Thrones: one in the House of Lords, two in Westminster Abbey and six in Buckingham Palace.

3/4 oz Whisky
3/4 oz Brandy
3/4 oz Benedictine
1/2 orange juice
1/2 lemon juice
Club Soda

Rinse out that shaker and here we go again. Shake the aforementioned ingredients together with ice until frothy cold. Strain the mixture over shaved ice into a Collins glass and top up with club soda where you will swizzle the drink for a few seconds. You may garnish with an orange and lemon slice and continue to repeat these steps in 5-10 minutes.

The Olympic

1 oz Brandy
1 oz Triple Sec
1 oz orange juice
orange peel

Shake shake shake, shake shake shake, shake your booty! In that ice-filled friendly shaker, froth the ingredients until the shaker becomes frosty cold. Strain into an already chilled Martini or cocktail glass and garnish with an orange peel. Remember, one is never enough, so invest in a larger shaker to limit physical fatigue.

FUN FACTS

Always making history, 1982 was no exception when Pope John Paul II visited Britain. He was the first Pope to do so for 450 years, in which the Queen, Titular Head of the Church of England, received him at Buckingham Palace.

It is said that Her Majesty keeps a yellow rubber duck and an inflatable crown in her bath.

1 oz ≈ 30 ml

Her Majesty's Reply to the Loyal Addresses of Parliament

Westminster Hall, Tuesday 20 March 2012

"My Lords and Members of the House of Commons, I am most grateful for your Loyal Addresses and the generous words of the Lord Speaker and Mr Speaker. This great institution has been at the heart of the country and the lives of our people throughout its history. As Parliamentarians, you share with your forebears a fundamental role in the laws and decisions of your own age.

Parliament has survived as an unshakeable cornerstone of our constitution and our way of life. History links monarchs and Parliament, a connecting thread from one period to the next. So in an era when the regular, worthy rhythm of life is less eye-catching than doing something extraordinary, I am reassured that I am merely the second Sovereign to celebrate a Diamond Jubilee.

As today, it was my privilege to address you during my Silver and Golden Jubilees. Many of you were present ten years ago and some of you will recall the occasion in 1977. Since my Accession, I have been a regular visitor to the Palace of Westminster and at the last count, have had the pleasurable duty of treating with twelve Prime Ministers.

Over such a period, one can observe that the experience of venerable old age can be a mighty guide but not a prerequisite for success in public office. I am therefore very pleased to be addressing many younger Parliamentarians and also those bringing such a wide range of background and experience to your vital, national work.

During these years as your Queen, the support of my family has, across the generations, been beyond measure. Prince Philip is, I believe, well-known for declining compliments of any kind. But throughout he has been a constant strength and guide. He and I are very proud and grateful that The Prince of Wales and other members of our family are travelling on my behalf in this Diamond Jubilee year to visit all the Commonwealth Realms and a number of other Commonwealth countries.

These overseas tours are a reminder of our close affinity with the Commonwealth, encompassing about one-third of the world's population. My own association with the Commonwealth has taught me that the most important contact between nations is usually contact between its peoples. An organisation dedicated to certain values, the Commonwealth has flourished and grown by successfully promoting and protecting that contact.

At home, Prince Philip and I will be visiting towns and cities up and down the land. It is my sincere hope that the Diamond Jubilee will be an opportunity for people to come together in a spirit of neighbourliness and celebration of their own communities.

We also hope to celebrate the professional and voluntary service given by millions of people across the country who are working for the public good. They are a source of vital support to the welfare and well-being of others, often unseen or overlooked.

And as we reflect upon public service, let us again be mindful of the remarkable sacrifice and courage of our Armed Forces. Much may indeed have changed these past sixty years but the valour of those who risk their lives for the defence and freedom of us all remains undimmed.

The happy relationship I have enjoyed with Parliament has extended well beyond the more than three and a half thousand Bills I have signed into law. I am therefore very touched by the magnificent gift before me, generously subscribed by many of you. Should this beautiful window cause just a little extra colour to shine down upon this ancient place, I should gladly settle for that.

We are reminded here of our past, of the continuity of our national story and the virtues of resilience, ingenuity and tolerance which created it. I have been privileged to witness some of that history and, with the support of my family, re-dedicate myself to the service of our great country and its people now and in the years to come."

Royal Vodka Drinks

There's no absolutes in life – only vodka.

Mick Jagger, The Rolling Stones

It was during the days of 'Red America' that contemporaries 'modernised' the Martini as well as several drink recipes with the introduction of Vodka. This mainly Eastern European spirit was rarely ever imbibed from the European continent before the 1950s, however in a few short years sales of Vodka in America topped that of bourbon by 1975. Progressing through the following years Vodka continued to rise in popularity eventually being used in favourite drinks such as Bloody Marys, Screwdrivers, several Martinis, etc. Vodka began to replace Gin in Martinis along with several cocktails, soon becoming a favourite in bars as well as in the societies that frequented them. According to the Gin and Vodka Association, Vodka was first distilled in 1174 at Khylnovsk, Russia as reported by the Vyatka Chronical, though scholars debate that it could have been distilled as early as the 8th century in Poland.

Vodka is produced by distilling fermented products such as grains, fruits, potatoes and sugars. Today's most popular Vodkas are produced from grains including but not limited to corn, rye and wheat, whereas other forms of Vodka are made from distilling grapes, molasses, potatoes, sugar beets and sometimes from odd resources such as wood pulp and by-products from oil refining. As one of the world's most favoured spirits, Vodka in its traditional form possessed an alcohol content of 38% by volume, whereas modern Vodka sees a 40% alcohol by volume (ABV) in nations such as Russia, Belarus, Poland, the Ukraine and Lithuania. The European Union dictates an ABV of 37.5%, whilst the United States dictates an ABV of 40% or more in order for Vodka to be named as such.

American and European Vodkas are known for their extensive filtration techniques before processing and the incorporation of flavoured additives, whilst traditional techniques use precise and exact distillation methods with limited filtering which preserves certain aspects and characteristics of its natural flavours. Filtering Vodka is often completed in stills during and after distillation where the spirit can further be filtered through other items such as charcoal which allows the absorption of alternative substances which alter the flavour of Vodka.

It is not uncommon for Vodka to be distilled multiple times or distilled in a fractioning still which not only improves the taste of the spirit but enhances its clarity. Water is Vodka's main dilutive as the spirit is distilled until it is almost pure alcohol where the water added determines the final alcohol content and flavour of the spirit depending on origins of the water. There are two classifications of Vodka: Clear Vodka and Flavoured Vodka in which Flavoured Vodkas can further be classified in two categories: Anniversary Vodka and Pepper Vodka. Most Vodka is unflavoured but Flavoured Vodkas are still produced in the same traditional way as their non-flavoured counterparts. Most times flavoured additives such as fruit flavouring, red pepper, ginger, chocolate, cinnamon and vanilla helped mask the medicinal attributes of the spirit's natural flavour such as Vodkas made for medicinal purposes in the Ukraine which contained St. John's Wort. Other such Vodkas contain grasses, honey, spices, herbs and roots. This favoured and often times fruity-flavoured spirit is traditionally drank neat in Eastern Europe which is traditionally known as the Vodka Belt. It is also commonly used in various mixed drinks and cocktails, and the Vodka Tonic has often rivalled the Gin and Tonic as a favoured summer refresher.

St George's Chapel

Also known as **Fuzzy Navel**

2 oz Vodka
1 oz Peach Schnapps
3 oz orange juice

In a Collins glass filled with ice, add the ingredients and swizzle the mixture until evenly distributed. Garnish with a peach slice. Fuzzy in the name refers to the peach, and naval to the orange, but I have been told by some of my Royal Navy friends that with enough of these drinks, you may wake up with a fuzzy naval "officer".

In addition to racing, the Queen also takes a keen interest in horse breeding. Horses bred at the Royal studs over the last 200 years have won virtually every major race in Britain. The Queen has about 25 horses in training each season.

QUOTE

"Work is the rent you pay for the room you occupy on earth."

Queen Elizabeth II

1 oz ≈ 30 ml

Admiralty Arch

Also known as Long Island Iced Tea

FUN FACT

In July of 2002, Her Majesty visited a mosque for the first time in the UK whilst visiting Scunthorpe, Lincolnshire.

QUOTE

"We lost the American colonies because we lacked the statesmanship to know the right time and the manner of yielding what is impossible to keep."

Queen Elizabeth II

1/2 oz Vodka
1/2 oz Gin
1/2 oz Blanco Tequila
1/2 oz Light Rum
1/2 oz Cointreau
1/2 oz lemon juice
4 oz Cola
lemon wedge

Pour all ingredients (with the exception of Cola and the lemon wedge) into a shaker almost filled with ice and shake vigorously until frothy cold. Strain the mixture into an ice-filled Collins glass and slowly top off with Cola. Garnish with the lemon wedge and indulge in this warming drink. A popular alternative to Afternoon Blend.

Gloriana

Also known as **Black Russian Cocktail**

2 oz Vodka
1 oz Kahlua

Simply stated, pour the ingredients into a highball glass filled with ice and stir. If preferred, add ingredients into a shaker with ice and shake until frothy cold and strain into a rocks glass. There is not much to this recipe but to enjoy it for all its worth!

1 oz ≈ 30 ml

HM Corgis

Also known as Salty Dog Cocktail

FUN FACTS

Her Majesty has a keen interest in horses and more importantly, horse racing. Her Majesty's first pony was a Shetland named Peggy, which was given to her by her grandfather, King George V, when she was four years old. The Queen continues to ride at Sandringham, Balmoral and Windsor.

On her honeymoon at Lord Mountbatten's country estate, Broadlands, Her Majesty had no less than 15 suitcases, whilst Prince Philip had just two.

2 1/2 oz Vodka
4 oz grapefruit juice
crushed sea salt
1 lime wedge

To prepare this highball glass, rim the lip with a lime wedge and dip the glass into crushed sea salt, thus creating a salted crust on the glass. Add a few large ice cubes into the glass and pour the Vodka and juice over the ice. Make sure to swizzle well and use the leftover lime wedge as garnish.
*Modify this drink by adding ¼ oz Maraschino Cherry Liqueur, which will allow people who appreciate grapefruit juice to enjoy this drink without its usual bitter flavour. Brilliant!

Bruton Street Belle

Also known as **Lemon Drop Cocktail**

2 oz Citrus-Infused Vodka
1/2 oz Cointreau
1/2 oz lemon juice
1/4 lemon
Granulated sugar

In the shaker filled with ice, add the Vodka, Cointreau and lemon juice. Shake vigorously until frothy and frosty cold, let sit for a few seconds to prepare the Martini glass. Rim the lip of the glass with a ¼ lemon and dip it into the granulated sugar crystals, thus creating a sweet crust on the rim of the glass. Pour the frothy mixture from the shaker into the chilled and prepared glass and serve with a slice of lemon. This drink is guaranteed to prevent scurvy!

FUN FACTS

The Queen's wedding ring was made from a nugget of Welsh gold which came from the Clogau St David's mine near Dolgellau. The ring of Prince Williams's wife, Catherine, Duchess of Cambridge also has a ring made of Welsh gold.

At a fancy dress party in her wedding year, Her Majesty dressed as a maid, whilst Prince Philip dressed as a waiter.

1 oz ≈ 30 ml

The Lady of London

Also known as **Cosmopolitan Cocktail**

2 oz Citron Vodka
1/2 oz Cointreau
1/2 oz lime juice
1/2 oz cranberry juice

Pour the ingredients into our shaker which will be almost filled with ice. Shake it up like Parliament and Her Majesty's finances and strain into an already chilled Martini glass, imbibe quickly so as not to lose the chill of the drink. I highly suggest spacing out the consumption of this cocktail before you take to the cover of Cosmo like Burt Reynolds.

The Glass Coach

Also known as **Screwdriver Cocktail**

2 1/2 oz Vodka
4 oz orange juice
1 orange twist

In a tall slender cocktail glass filled with ice, pour the Vodka and orange juice so that the ice is completely covered. Swizzle this mixture until evenly dispersed and add the orange twist as garnish. This drink reportedly obtained its name in Saudi Arabia as American engineers secretly added Vodka to their orange juice and swizzled them with their screwdrivers.

Bloody Queen Mary

FUN FACTS

In addition to her corgis and dorgis, the Queen also breeds and trains Labradors and Cocker Spaniels at Sandringham. There is a special Sandringham strain of black Labrador which was founded in 1911.

Her Majesty's pet name is "Sausage", as Prince Philip likes to call her.

2 oz Vodka
4 oz tomato juice
1/2 oz lemon juice (some prefer lime juice)
1/4 tsp ground black pepper
1/4 oz Worcestershire sauce
1 dash of Tabasco sauce
1 dash of celery salt
1 medium stalk of celery

In our trusty shaker, shake all of the ingredients (of course we do not include the celery at this point) with ice until frothy cold. Continue by straining the mixture into a Collins glass filled with ice and then add the celery stalk to the glass as garnish. This drink is perfect for the morning after you have imbibed the other drinks in this book, unless you have a keen feeling to know how Bloody Mary's (Mary I) prisoners felt whilst imprisoned in the Tower.

EIIR, From Princess to Queen

Written in honour of Her Majesty,
the Queen's 60th anniversary of Her accession
6, February 2012

1952–2012

Long ago are the days of old, when débutantes were presented to the palace, social graces and manners were common place, deference towards the crown was high and the masses understood the saying, "for Crown and country"! Much like society has drastically changed over the last 60 years, as has the life of an innocent little girl who became Queen by the decision of one man who chose his feelings over his duty. As time has passed and many have gone that remember the abdication crisis of 1936, it was this singular event in our history that has shaped the woman we know today as our Queen. Though born a Princess on 21, April 1926, Elizabeth's early years were as normal as could be. Being born royal of course would provide a comfortable life but being born to the brother of the heir to the throne would leave Elizabeth out of the formal expectations and pressures that would accompany and be expected of those born directly to the heir apparent.

The formal duties and functions of State would not be of worry or even thought about by a person born into Elizabeth's position within her family. The first of her generation to be born (Granddaughter of King George V and niece of the heir to the throne), Elizabeth was not just a famous baby but third in line to the throne at this time, as her Uncle David (The Prince of Wales) had not yet married or produced heirs of his own. As the years went by and little Elizabeth advanced in age she enjoyed the comforts of a safe and secure family life shielded from the public trappings and confines of a demanding public life. The odd sitting for a portrait or photograph popped up every now and again but that was no different in those days as taking family photos are to us today. She continued to be known as the world's most famous child as she grew; as her Uncle had still not married and no other children (besides Princess Margaret in 1930) of her generation were born to any other members of the immediate Royal family.

Just a girl in 1936 when her Grandfather King George V died, it must have been difficult for a ten-year old to fully comprehend the decision that her uncle

(King Edward VIII) would make only a few short months later, to abdicate his throne which would ultimately and dramatically change her life as she was to know it. Moving from a modest London townhouse and into the large rooms of Buckingham Palace would be overwhelming for any child but the chaos she was thrust into was not to end, but to grow into a way of life that would define her character for her entire life to come. Losing more than just her childhood home, it was her family that would suffer the greatest change and eventual loss in the coming years. Though a favourite of her Grandparents King George V and Queen Mary, little Elizabeth (known as Lilibet to her family) was not exposed to the greater extent of Royal life, as her own small family was mostly removed from the high demand and public profile associated with royal duties. Elizabeth's father (Prince Albert, or Bertie to his family) suffered from a stammer, and it was her mother's reluctance to a royal life that contributed to the refusal of Prince Albert's advances and several marriage proposals.

Knowing what would be expected of her in a "Royal" marriage and life, Elizabeth Bowes-Lyon denied acceptance of the man she loved, however it was that same love that eventually saw the Duke's advances accepted and his last proposal succeed. Elizabeth was comforted by the fact that the Duke's difficulties with public speaking kept him from a great expanse of public duty, and also knowing that his brother would become king, further put her mind at ease knowing she would not have to endure the demanding life of being constantly in the public eye. Elizabeth was of Scottish aristocracy, however she was not royal. This did not prove an issue as she was the first non-Royal to be accepted and eventually marry into the immediate Royal family. After their wedding, the Duke and his new Duchess of York welcomed their first daughter Elizabeth, followed by another beautiful girl named Margaret four years later. The York Household enjoyed a happy time of low profile "royal" life within their small family, which was simply referred to as "us four" by Prince Albert, Duke of York. When duties were asked of the Yorks, it was often times the Duchess who had to step into the role on behalf of her husband due to increased difficulties with his stammer that made the duties of public life for him stressful. There were no major expectations from senior members of the Royal family or highly important public duties expected of the York family (with an exception now and again) because it was little Elizabeth's uncle, not her father who was directly next in line to the throne.

It was not until the passing of little Elizabeth's Grandfather, King George V, that things started to become more turbulent within the royal family itself, which would start to invade the confines of the safety and comfort of the York way of life. As Elizabeth's uncle dangerously played with the monarchy's future and the love of a nation, it became increasingly apparent that the King cared little for his position, as he exerted little time or interest to what was expected of him. He did not take his new role seriously as he did not want to be King though his destiny was to see him as such. Adamantly choosing private desire over public duty, Edward VIII instigated a rift within his family which would take decades to resolve and an eternity to forgive. He was not seen as fit to reign, something that his father King George V knew. The King often discussed the irresponsible actions of his son, David, which proved to him and the family that the Prince of Wales was not fit for the heavy burden and duty associated with a stringent life as King. This was once again about to be proven to the world. With the abdication crisis unfolding along with growing tensions on the continent, Queen Mary, the York family and Palace courtiers saw the newly-ascended King Edward VIII frolic in a dangerous liaison with a twice-divorced American woman, Mrs Wallis Simpson. Foregoing his duty in favour of personal luxuries and comforts, along with his scandalous affair, the King set out to make Mrs. Simpson his wife which was highly controversial and frowned upon by the establishment. It was simply unprecedented. This was not something that the nation would take to, nor would it be allowed in the eyes of the Church in which he was 'Defender of the Faith'.

Knowing Mrs. Simpson had now filed for divorce, an ultimatum was presented to the King, in which he chose to relinquish his duties and abdicate his throne to be with the woman he loved.

Once the instrument of abdication was signed and witnessed, it was Albert, the reluctant Duke of York who would now be styled, His Majesty King George VI. The pressures of being King and the duties of sovereign were now to fall upon the Duke of York, who was always in a delicate state of health from his time as a child. Never meant to be king nor wanting to see himself or his family in this Royal role, King George VI knew that his life and that of his little daughters now belonged to the British people. As the former King (who was now styled as the Duke of Windsor) went into a life of banishment from the royal court and family, so too went the care-free life of the little Princess Elizabeth. Days of playing with her sister, being read stories by her father and enjoying a worry-free childhood, would soon be far and few in-between as a new life of being groomed as the heir to the throne would take precedence. Issues of State would soon come to take over her home and her life, as she would grow into the duty she has come to display today.

Her father was no longer solely hers, her sister's or her mother's as not only he, but her entire family now belonged to not just the nation but the Commonwealth too where duty trumped all else. The destiny that had been her father's would soon be realised by Princess Elizabeth, as special concessions would be made which would help keep Elizabeth closed off from a world outside of the Palace walls. Finding herself in a position very different from what she was used to, it was the abdication crisis which taught her the lessons of duty, honour and service which would ultimately become her trademark. Elizabeth would soon come to find that the destiny of her father would one day be hers too, as it would also be that of her own family and children in the years to come. Now King to his people at home and around the world, Elizabeth realised that her days of a quiet family upbringing were over as the duties of State consumed her father, the King and mother, the

Queen, and thrust her and her sister into the bright and very demanding public limelight. With the renouncement of duty, the discarding of the throne and a short stroke of a pen, King Edward VIII dramatically altered little Elizabeth's life by changing it a drastic 180 degrees. From a little girl at play forced into the direct responsibilities of State, Elizabeth and her sister were now two of the most famous girls in the world which the public would always be watching.

The Coronation of King George VI and Queen Elizabeth was attended by the Princesses Elizabeth and Margaret which would prove a great experience for her own Coronation. She was being exposed in full to the meanings and ways of Royal life, duty and protocol; something far removed from her previous Mayfair existence. However, the growing pressures of Royal life would eventually take its toll on her father the King. As the king grew in popularity as his reign advanced, the unity of 'us four' did not waver. Still wanting to retain as much normalcy as possible for his little girls, the Palace went through great lengths to keep the little Princesses safe and protected whilst offering them a very minimal taste of the opportunities of childhood outside of the palace. Trying to capture as much of a normal life as possible, Elizabeth and her sister joined the girl guides in which a troop was set up at Buckingham Palace for the little princesses to belong to. There were not a lot of children to play with at the Palace, therefore children and other girl guides from outside of the Palace were brought in to mingle with the princesses.

Continuing to improve his stammer, the King seemingly took to the task of his duty as Monarch. He was able to reach out to his people through speech, in which his actions as leader of the nation would say more than his words ever could. As if life had not changed enough for little Elizabeth and her family, the dark clouds of war would soon start to expand from the continent as Nazi Germany would soon threaten our shores. During these uncertain years, it was a brief encounter in 1939 at Dartmouth Naval College which would see Elizabeth grow into her own as a young lady, as she became royally smitten with a young naval cadet by the name of Prince Philip of Greece who had adopted the last name of his Uncle "Dickie" Mountbatten when he became a naturalised British subject. However the simple innocence of young love was to be overshadowed as the situation in Europe intensified. War was now inevitable and so started the preparations for battle. London's children were sent to the safety of the country, which also included Princess Elizabeth and her sister Princess Margaret who were evacuated to the safety of Windsor Castle (which was simply referred to as a 'house in the country'). Their parents, the King and Queen remained in residence at Buckingham Palace as a show of solidarity with their people.

As London was heavily bombed, Buckingham Palace itself was bombed no less than nine times during which Nazi bombs destroyed the Palace Chapel in 1940. Another bomb was dropped in the quadrangle whilst the King and Queen were in residence. Narrowly escaping, Their Majesties emerged from the broken Palace to shattered glass from blown-in windows and debris from the bombs explosions. As the King and Queen were filmed surveying the damage of their home, Her Majesty made a statement that was to become one of her most famous, "I am glad we have been bombed. Now I can look the East End in the face". Now that the Palace had endured such bombing as the other parts of London had during the war, Their Majesties were able to truly relate to and feel the pain of their subjects. Truly revered by the people for staying at the Palace and not abandoning the city of London for the safety of a secluded country estate, The King and Queen were seen to be sharing in the peoples hardship and pain as reported by The Sunday Graphic on 18, September 1939 (Page 1): "By the Editor: The King and Queen have endured the ordeal which has come to their subjects. For the second time a German bomber has tried to bring death and destruction to the home of Their Majesties...When this war is over the common danger which King George and Queen Elizabeth have shared with their people will be a cherished memory and an inspiration through the years." Being amongst the masses and sharing in their grief, endeared the King and Queen to their people. The Princesses spent much of the War at Windsor however they were still shown in their State capacity as making war-time speeches to the children of the nation and upon Princess Elizabeth's 16th Birthday she was inspecting her own regiment of Grenadier Guards in which she was Colonel.

In support of the war effort, it was Princess Elizabeth who was to set an example by training as a mechanic in the ATS. Here, she learned to drive and maintain various types of motor vehicles including those used for war. The Princess was often found working in overalls on the engines of Red Cross motor cars such as when her father, the King, came to visit her and observe whilst she was performing her duties. A few more years of uncertainty would pass before Prime Minister, Winston Churchill proclaimed an end to the war. It was on this day that he joined the King and the Royal family on the balcony of Buckingham Palace to the delight and cheers of the crowds that had gathered to celebrate the victory over Nazi Germany. As the celebrations of the day carried through into the night, the two little Princesses in disguise escaped the palace to join the throngs of people so they could for once in their lives enjoy a few hours of being a normal everyday person. Though the war had come to an end and Britain could start rebuilding, it was six years of war-stress and pressure that took its toll on the fragile health of our King. Such effects on His Majesty's mind and body left him significantly weaker but his belief in duty to his nation along with his strong will continued to see his reign successful.

After the war Prince Philip of Greece and Princess Elizabeth were seen together more frequently in society. Little was it known that during her time at Windsor Castle, the Princess had kept a photograph of Prince Philip with her. As they communicated, their liaisons became more and more frequent and a royal love affair blossomed. 1947 saw the first Royal tour taken with the entire Royal family in which the Princesses were off to enjoy the sights and experiences of South

Africa. Official duties were the priority of the King and Queen but for Princess Elizabeth this tour would also mark her 21st Birthday in which she made one of her most famous speeches to the Commonwealth of Nations. Taking time out from touring and safari, Princess Elizabeth took to the airwaves proclaiming, "I declare before you all, that my whole life whether it be long or short, shall be devoted to your service and the service of our great imperial family to which we all belong. But I shall not have strength to carry out this resolution alone unless you join in it with me, as I now invite you to do - I know that your support will be unfailingly given. God help me to make good my vow, and God bless all of you who are willing to share in it".

Now bound by duty for her entire life, the Princess was acting on the lessons which she had witnessed and was taught from childhood - duty first, self second. As Britain and the Commonwealth revelled in the Princesses Birthday speech, her homecoming would be made even happier as the announcement of her wedding engagement to Prince Philip was announced. It was later that year on the 20th of November 1947 saw the largest and most popular celebrations in Britain for decades. This union and this Royal Wedding was what the nation needed. It was a light emerging from the darkness of a war-ravaged Britain in which years of gloom and despair seemed to disappear as Princess Elizabeth and her new husband were the symbols of renewed hope, prosperity and continuity. They were described as a perfect couple in the eyes of the British media and their adoring public. After her wedding Princess Elizabeth happily agreed to take on more official duties to help lighten the load of her father's diary. As the King continued to become more feeble and his work- load dispersed more heavily in his heir's direction, his failing health was masked and kept from the public. Knowing that his daughter needed time with her new husband, the King offered Prince Philip a Naval command in Malta where Princess Elizabeth would join him not as heir to the throne but as a simple navy wife. It was in 1948 that the Princess gave birth to her first child, Prince Charles, and so began the happy days of the young family. However the family life that Princess Elizabeth was starting would not be what she herself had as a baby. The Princess was heir to the throne which meant she would have to protect and shield her family from the glare of the media and the public. There was no way around the duty to which she was bound therefore her children would often play second fiddle to the demands of State. Prince Philip began to reduce his role in the navy to take on more public duties with his wife on the King's behalf. He was very adamant about helping others and it was obvious that he could relate to people of all stations and make them comfortable in his presence. The royal couple were often away from home on official duty and whilst on an official visit to Canada in 1950 their second child, Princess Anne, was born. Although the royal couple now had two children, less time was actually allotted to being at home with them as their duties of State increased.

1952 saw a planned overseas Commonwealth tour for the King and Queen in which the Royal diary saw a most gruelling schedule. It was due to the fragile health of the King that Princess Elizabeth and Prince Philip agreed to embark on this tour to represent Their Majesties abroad. As the departure day arrived, King George VI, Queen Elizabeth and Princess Margaret saw Princess Elizabeth and her husband off from the tarmac at London Airport (Heathrow). This was not just a farewell until the Princess' return; it was to be a final goodbye from a father to his daughter. The King sent a Princess of the realm to represent him to the people of the Commonwealth, knowing that she would return a Queen. Whilst on her tour in Kenya, on 6 February 1952, the Princess received the heart-wrenching news that His Majesty the King, had died peacefully in his sleep. She immediately returned home as Queen to her people. It was here in Kenya that she decided to be addressed by her own name, thus styled Queen Elizabeth II. Upon her return to London, Winston Churchill along with several Privy Councillors met the new Queen at Heathrow where she famously exclaimed at the sight of

them, "Oh, they have sent the hearses!" But there was no time for her to grieve on her own as the daughter of a beloved father; the new Queen's first official duty was to lead her great nation in mourning for her father the late King George VI at his funeral. King George VI was greatly admired, loved and endeared to his people for his bravery and steadfast war-time attitude. His funeral was attended by his brother the Duke of Windsor but not his sister-in-law the Duchess as she was not welcome. The Duke was never forgiven by Her Majesty the Queen Mother, as it was seen that the abdication which thrust the Duke of York to the forefront of duty as the reluctant King George VI, had indeed cost him his life in which he was taken much to early from her, his family and now his people.

Queen Elizabeth II watched the position her father never wanted, send him to an untimely death but it was his spirit and sense of duty that was impressed on the young and dutiful Queen. The event of the King's passing had a profound effect upon the new Queen and her family, as Prince Philip left his aspiring and successful naval career to work alongside his wife, the Queen, as her support and consort. The summer of 1953 saw a coronation of unparalleled excitement and celebration throughout London as the glamour and youth of the new queen was attractive to the nation, where London itself was again young, lively and full of hope. The death of Queen Mary at the start of the year signified the passing of the old guard in which a new age and style of monarchy would emerge to truly reflect Britain. Change was occurring and renewed hope was already high in spirit as the Queen agreed for television cameras to be granted access to the Coronation ceremony which would allow millions of her new subjects to bear witness to her crowning. This was a clean break from what the old guard would have decided which would have been to keep the television cameras out of the ceremony altogether. The ceremony itself was of tremendous pomp, glamour and spectacle which saw Prince Philip pledge his allegiance to his wife as his 'God anointed Queen' and her 'liege man of life and limb'.

The Coronation of such a young, energetic and lively Queen was the moment in our history which assured that change was welcomed and was going to happen within this new Elizabethan era. In the months to come, Her Majesty along with Prince Philip would embark on a six-month long tour which was designed to help save the Commonwealth by bolstering support for the institution of monarchy whilst using the popularity of the new Queen and her husband to do so. This tour helped create the Commonwealth as we know it today; but not before the christening of the Royal Yacht Britannia was completed which would serve the Queen for over 40-plus years before being decommissioned by Tony Blair's Labour government in 1997. This Coronation tour saw the Queen cover over 50K miles to far-away realms and back where she would bear witness to a variety of cultures and languages which comprised the vast complexity of her overseas realms. Upon her visit to New Zealand, she opened parliament for the first time in her reign, an historic visit in that it was the first time a reigning monarch had presided over such a session there. As the Queen returned home to vast cheering throngs of her subjects, she was greeted by none other than the Queen Mother, her sister Princess Margaret and her Prime Minister Winston Churchill aboard Britannia. She was driven by horse and carriage through the cheering city streets of London to lunch and then home to Buckingham Palace and the rest is royal history!

Her Majesty may be constant, but sure and steady is something of a controversial and contrary statement. The Queen is the only monarch in the history of Britain to instigate and complete such radical change over such long periods of time within an institution that some continue to perceive and promote as archaic and useless in today's modern world. In 1952, Her Majesty came to head an institution unchanged since the days of King Edward VII which was very stiff and regulated by unwavering tradition with an almost arrogant aloofness. As a new Queen for a new time saw a world changing from the end of WWII, Her Majesty has ushered out old, stuffy court traditions and has breathed new life into what many call "the establishment". It is the Queen who has welcomed change to her public life during the last 60 years and has not only changed herself but the institution of the crown itself which defines us as a people. Her Majesty serves as an example to the nation as she has found a way over the last several decades to intertwine both her official and formal roles with her informal and candid experiences to become a true symbol and reflection of Britain in the 21st century. She has strived to change the Monarchy for the better, making it adaptable and truly reflective of a modern and constantly-changing Britain. She is the personification of the State in all its glory, truly a symbol of the might and majesty of our past, present and future as a nation. It has been decades of domestic and international experience, service and duty which have endeared her to the people of not only our realm but the realms and dominions overseas which treasure and value her in many of the same ways we do here at home.

In the beginning of her reign, 'duty and dedication' superseded everything, even her own family. However, after much practice as a Princess and phenomenal experience as sovereign, the hardships she endured and crises she triumphed over has seen her single-handedly reformulate the equation of duty and service within the growing informality of the modern world. During her reign the monarchy has seen its ups and downs and it has been the Queen who has tightened the reins and welcomed the change which would ultimately direct the crown to be the open and transparent institution we know and love. The Queen has triumphed over turmoil, loss, and tides of republicanism during each decade of the last 60 years as reflected in the 1990s when Her Majesty faced the most trying and troubling times of her reign. Describing 1992 as her "Annus Horribilis", Her Majesty witnessed the breakdown of two of her own children's marriages which were shrouded in scandal; and a fire which gutted much of her childhood home to name a few downs of the decade. She embraced the truths of both faltering marriages and made the difficult decisions to see both of Prince Charles' and Prince Andrew's marriages dissolved. As Windsor Castle was uninsured, Her Majesty faced public scrutiny over taxpayers footing the bill to repair the Castle. She made the hefty decision to open the Castle as well as Buckingham Palace to the public in order to raise the funds to repair the rooms which were devastated by the fire as well as paying a vast sum towards the repairs out of her own private funds. 1992 was not a year that the Queen would look upon favourably but little did she know that this decade of her reign was to see more trying times for the House of Windsor.

The turning point of Her Majesty's reign which saw the greatest amount of change toward the formal portrayal of the crown was the death of Princess Diana. Though she may hold many important titles and honours which are celebrated and revered, 1997 was a year that saw large throngs of people care little for formality and duty whilst demanding more "feeling" and "spectacle" from the establishment and Her Majesty the Queen. As the saga of the death of Princess Diana was quickly spread by the media, Her Majesty did not stand a chance against the onslaught of public grief and anger that was driven like wildfire from the very outlet that helped create and ultimately destroy the Princess of Wales.

The nation has always rallied around the Queen in both times of good and bad, however this particular event saw the Queen used as a scapegoat for the grief, sense of loss and pain which many transformed into anger and raw emotion that they directed not only towards the institution but the Queen herself. Not understanding this sensational change in her people, Her Majesty could not get her head around the changes which were suggested by Her government that would in fact help ease the public's fury and emotional charge. Traditions that have been with the crown for centuries were now facing extreme change which was something the Queen had to face. She did what she had to do and yielded against her judgement to keep the integrity of the crown intact and stable for the future of the nation. Her Majesty directed a flag be flown at half-mast over the palace which has never been done before, her summer holiday tending to her grieving grandchildren cut short to be with her people in London and a televised tribute to Diana which culminated in a bow to her coffin on the day of her funeral as the cortège passed the palace.

Now leading her people through their grief, Her Majesty was able to overcome this seemingly desperate time of troubled popularity. Changing in the ways that best-suited the people and the establishment was something that the Queen had to do to further protect the institution that supersedes even her authority. Again her sense of duty prevailed and all was made right with her people. Her Majesty had shown not just the nation but the world as a whole that she is in fact adaptable with the times. Her Majesty is not the staunch, resistant to change, out of touch monarch she has been painted to be by certain organisations. In fact, it is Her Majesty who has initiated the greatest amount of change within the establishment in order to be closer to her people, and more in tune with the modern thoughts and beliefs of how government is handled and operated. From the archaic institution she inherited has come the efficient, open, and 'feeling' monarchy that people have come to cherish and need. Somewhere along the last 60 years of her reign, the public transition from ideology and example, to feelings and emotions seemed to have caught the Queen off-guard as this was exemplified during the late summer days of 1997.

Since the seemingly dark days of the 1990s, the Queen has enjoyed a large period of increasing popularity. Events such as the millennium celebrations, her Golden Jubilee celebrations along with Royal tours, as well as the many Royal weddings that have taken place have put Her Majesty at the top of her game. The crown and more importantly Her Majesty, in particular, is more popular now than she has ever been. She is a revered Stateswoman with a very important title but behind all of that is just a woman who has made do with what life has given her. She is kind and generous, able to relate to her people no matter their station in life. She is a loved and loving member of her family who has openly been seen laughing

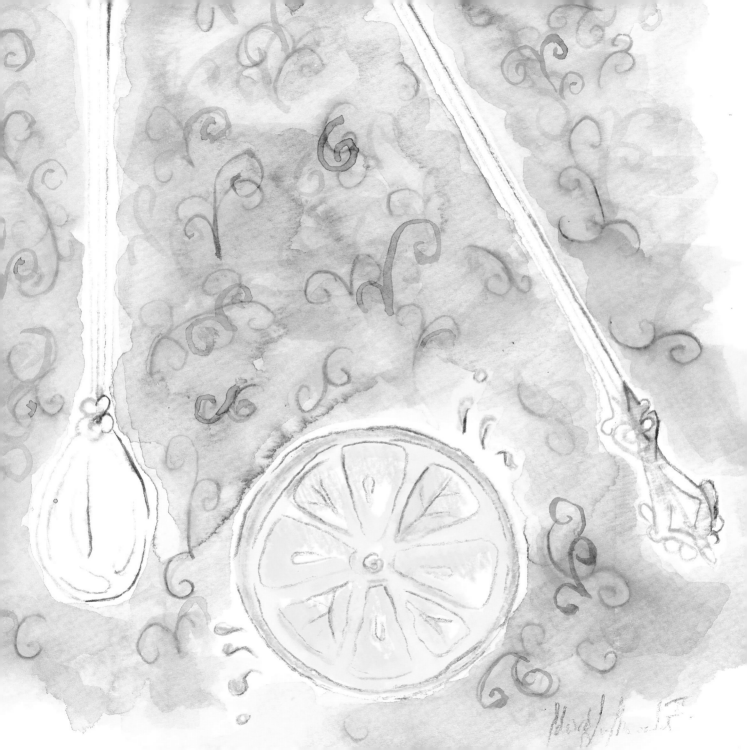

and crying as well as joking in public and in private. She has taken an official role and made it less stuffy and 'stiff upper-lipped' whilst showing the world that she too is a woman of feelings and warm-heartedness.

Most importantly after 60 years, Her Majesty is a living national treasure unto herself, and a fitting example as to what and who we are as a people. There may have been times of indifference to the crown and the Queen but the last few years have seen change, as a growing wave of younger generations are endearing the Queen to their hearts. Again there is deference to the crown and this institution which has changed greatly over the last 60 years which has brought renewed popularity to our people, our culture and the traditions which have identified our islands to the outside world. With the rise in the popularity of the crown and the Queen in particular, has emerged the pro-monarchy and pro-education organisations which see their duty to defend, protect and promote the integrity of the Crown at home and around the world. Such groups as the British Monarchist Society and Defenders of the Crown here at home as well as similar organisations across the seas in Her Majesty's realms of Canada (Monarchist League of Canada), Australia (Australians for Constitutional Monarchy and the Australian Monarchist League) , New Zealand (Monarchy New Zealand), the Caribbean (the Caribbean Monarchist League) and Jamaica (Jamaica Monarchist League) have vowed to continue educating the people about monarchy, its role and its relevance in the modern world. Along with dedication to the crown of such organisations they have also vowed to rise up and defend the crown against the offensive and destructive assault of the republican movement. It is not only the education of the crown and its role which will see the lasting existence of this great institution, it is the ways in which the establishment is able to change to meet the needs and desires of the people that will see it endure the decades and centuries to come. As Her Majesty has been at the helm of great change in a seemingly unforgiving world we are approving, grateful, respectful and loving of this woman who has pledged her entire life to our service. She has reigned brilliantly over the years with our best interests in mind and heart whilst representing us without a blemish to a world that still emulates and looks to the United Kingdom in many different aspects of modern life. It is not with just the support of her Husband and family that see her successful in her duties but the support of her people at home and across the seas that love, revere and respect her.

As politicians have come and gone and the times have changed with each passing decade, it is Her Majesty who has harnessed and implemented the many changes which have endeared the institution of monarchy to us the people. From an innocent and protected little Princess rose and evolved a Stateswoman of stature that braved the perils of family battle, the evils of war, the death of her loved ones and the many events which tried her patience and faith during the last 60 years of her reign. It has been this new Elizabethan age which has seen the fabric of British society tested and tried whilst great change has been implemented for the betterment of Her people. Looking back on a job that was never meant to be hers it can truly be said that Elizabeth II has triumphed in every way over the many hurdles and obstacles that have been placed in her way. From tiara to Imperial State Crown it is with great pride and respect that we recognise the efforts of this magnificent woman who evolved from Princess to Queen.

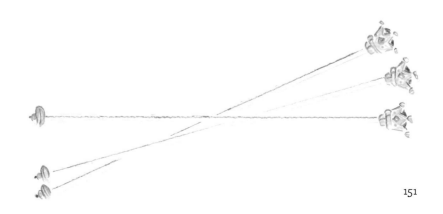

Royal Champagne Drinks

My only regret in life is that I did not drink more Champagne.

John Maynard Keynes (1883–1946) English Economist

Yes, it is French but it was an Englishman who invented and perfected the method by which Champagne is now known. Despite English advancements in the methods of creating Champagne and though it be little known to the masses. "Brut" Champagne was intentionally created for the British market in 1846 by Perrier-Jouët. In diversifying his production of champagne (in which sweet champagne was the style of the day), Perrier-Jouët on purpose did not sweeten the beverage before its transport to England, thus creating the Champagne which is most often drank today. Being ever so tasty, some call it 'sparkling wine' but in the true spirit of this alcohol 'Champagne' is ever so fitting as it is a reflection of the lustre associated with symbols of luxury and the elite as the French intended. It was not until the mid 19th century that Champagne became one of the most popular beverages in the world. It began in the mid 1800s and truly exploded during the 'belle-epoque' at the end of the century. In fact, Champagne greatly rose in popularity and exportation from as many as 20 million bottles being produced in 1850 as opposed to the marginal 300,000 bottles produced in 1800. Today an average of 330 million bottles of Champagne is produced annually, proving that Champagne has continued its trend as being a popular beverage through the years.

Champagne became popular due to its close association with the anointment of the Kings of France in which the crowned heads of Europe and their courts helped promote this crisp refreshing drink as the beverage most closely associated with luxury and power. Champagne by definition is "a sparkling wine produced by inducing 'in-bottle secondary fermentation'" of the wine to effect carbonation. The term "Champagne" is used to refer to wine produced exclusively within the Champagne region of France, from which it takes its name. In previous centuries and even today have seen superior manufacturers of Champagne staunchly devoted to creating a history and further more an identity for their brand of 'sparkling wine'. These producers have played on the history of Champagne and have further associated themselves with it, with the expectation of driving their name and product to the top by using the exclusive attraction of royalty and nobility along with synonyms such as luxury, festivity and special occasion.

Champagne's base is of grapes which are normally those used to create Pinot Noir, Pinot Gris, Chardonnay and Pinot Meunier. The laws of appellation (region) for Champagne only allows the use of grapes which are grown in specifically designated areas within the appellation to be considered and used for the production of Champagne. These rules are bound through international treaty as well as French national law and other regulations which limit the term Champagne to be used only by those varieties of wine products that come from the Champagne appellation. The European Union also ardently restricts the use of the term Champagne unless it is from the Champagne region whereas in America, the government maintains regulations that allow its own producers of 'sparkling wine' to use the term Champagne under special circumstances.

Almost all of the producers in America refer to Champagne as 'sparkling wine' and the name itself is not used on their labels or as is the case in certain states, producers are forbidden by law to refer to their product as 'Champagne'. Champagne is usually served in its own glass known as a Champagne Flute which is identified by its long tall hollow stem and narrow bowl of thin sides. Champagne is best served cold; an ideal serving temperature (drinking) temperature should be between 7 and 9 degrees C (45 to 48 degrees F). Champagne should always be chilled appropriately before serving therefore if it has not come out of a cooler or household refrigerator it is recommended it is chilled in a bath of ice water in a Champagne Bucket to minimize the possibility of a gassy expulsion and overflow when opening.

Though the French are credited with the development of Champagne it was the Romans who planted the vast vineyards in the north-east area of France where grape cultivation for the making of wine dates to around the 5th century. Beginning before and continuing through medieval times, it was the churches which owned and operated the vast majority of vineyards to make wines for the Eucharist. The monks were traditionally responsible for the production of such alcohol. As French Kings traditionally were anointed in Reims it was wines from the Champagne region which were served as part of the coronation festivities further advancing the region as a popular and posh wine-making region.

The first account of the creation of a sparkling wine (a Blanquette de Limoux) was by the Benedictine Monks of the Abbey of Saint Hilaire near Carcassonne in 1531, therefore disproving the popular belief that Dom Perignon was the father of such a wine even though he may have popularised and advanced the production of the beverage. Dom Perignon made contributions to the production of Champagne such as inventing the wiring that holds the cork in place to withstand the gasses of fermentation. Though Dom Perignon is often mistakenly coined the father of Champagne it was an English Scientist by the name of Mr. Christopher Merret, that formulated the second fermentation of the wine by adding sugar to the mixture; this happened to be decades before Dom Perignon visited his place of Champagne production (the Abbey of Hautvillers). In 1662 Mr Merret was credited with his advances in Champagne production due to the fact that he provided written documents of his experiments with the production of Champagne to the Royal Society in which he explained his findings and the advancement of the beverage itself with the Champagne Method (or Methode Champenoise).

The méthode champenoise begins with still wine fermented from the aforementioned grapes, which is the base of Champagne. As this is the secondary fermentation, yeast and sugar are added to the wine which is then bottled and capped, not corked. The wine mixture is allowed to ferment for 2 to 3 weeks or longer, which can sometimes be from several months to several years. During this process of fermentation the yeast reacts with the sugar in the bottle which results in the trapping of carbon dioxide in the bottle. It is when the second fermentation and the resting period are both finished that the yeast and remaining sediment must be removed from the bottle. The bottles' sediment contents are removed when the bottles are positioned on a 'riddling rack' which allows the refermented wine to be rotated at a slow speed from a horizontal to vertical position thus allowing the sediment to move into the neck of the bottle for easy extraction, termed 'disgorgement'. Once this sediment is removed a small amount of champagne is added to fill the space for 'topping' off the bottle. It is then corked and the wire netting called a 'muselet' is put in place to keep the contents securely contained within the highly pressurised bottle.

Buckingham Palace Garden

Also known as Queen's Cousin Cocktail

1 oz Vodka
1/2 oz Grand Marnier
1/2 oz of fresh lime juice
1 tsp Triple Sec
Champagne
2 dashes Bitters

In a shaker, bring the Vodka, Grand Marnier, Triple Sec and lime juice to a frigid froth. Pour this mixture into a large Champagne flute and top gracefully with Champagne. Serve with 2 dashes of Bitters.

FUN FACTS

In the summer of 2005, The Queen opened the first "children's trail" in the Buckingham Palace garden for the Summer Opening.

Her Majesty (when in argument with her husband Prince Philip) will often speak in riddles to confuse his thinking and logic.

1 oz ≈ 30 ml

Buckingham's Gate

FUN FACT

Her Majesty's official wedding cake was made by McVitie and Price Ltd using ingredients given as a wedding gift by Australian Girl Guides.

QUOTE

"It is as Queen of Canada that I am here. Queen of Canada and all Canadians, not just one or two ancestral strains."

Queen Elizabeth II

3 1/2 oz Hypnotiq
3 oz Champagne
1/2 oz Grenadine

In the shaker, bring the Hypnotiq and grenadine to a chilled frothy mixture. In a chilled Champagne flute, pour in the ice-cold Champagne followed by a slow steady pour of the Hypnotiq and Grenadine mixture. Garnish with strawberry if desired.

Kensington Palace

1 oz Melon Liqueur
1/3 oz Sweet and Sour Mix
4 oz Champagne

In a tall chilled Champagne flute, pour the Melon Liqueur together with the sweet and sour mix into the flute, top with Champagne and garnish with fresh melon slices.

1 oz ≈ 30 ml

FUN FACT

The Queen's real birthday is on 21, April, but is officially celebrated on the second Saturday of June. The reason for an official Birthday in June actually dates back to the early 1800s where the Birthday of the Sovereign was moved to early summer to take advantage of better weather. Her Majesty celebrates her actual Birthday in a low-key fashion; however her official Birthday is a different matter. Celebrated with parades, massed bands and a Royal Air Force flyover. Her Majesty presides over Trooping the Colour and presents new colours to a chosen regiment. She also spends time with her family on the balcony of Buckingham Palace greeting the crowds who have come to give their best wishes. The day's events are concluded with a 21-gun salute in Green Park along with a coloured flight of red, white and blue by the Red Arrows.

QUOTE

"These wretched babies don't come until they are ready."

Queen Elizabeth II

The Princess Margaret

3 1/2 oz Champagne
1 oz Gold Rum
1 oz orange juice (with pulp)
1/2 oz lemon juice
1/4 oz Grenadine syrup

Using your shaker filled with ice, shake all of the ingredients (sans Champagne) until the shaker is riddled with frost. Strain the mixture into a large white wine glass and top off with Champagne. Serve with a lemon and orange peel as garnish.

The Garter Star

Also known as Champagne Cocktail

1 cube sugar
Bitters
chilled Champagne

Soak the sugar cube with a couple of good splashes of Bitters and place in the bottom of a large Champagne flute. Fill slowly with sparkling wine. Garnish with a lemon twist.

The Queen has owned over 30 corgis during her reign. Her first was Susan who was a present for her 18th birthday. Her Majesty currently has five corgis at her feet by the names of Emma, Linnet, Monty, Holly and Willow. Her Majesty is credited with the breed "Dorgi", which is a cross between a Corgi and a Dachshund. Cider, Berry, Vulcan and Candy, all Dorgis, keep the Queen's corgis company.

Her Majesty carries in her purse a wedding gift Prince Philip gave to her, a silver make-up case.

1 oz ≈ 30 ml

RVO (Royal Victorian Order)

Also known as Magna Carta Cocktail

FUN FACTS

Her Majesty is the first member of the British Royal Family to ever be awarded a gold disc from the recording industry. 100,000 copies of the CD of the 'Party at the Palace' produced by EMI, were sold within the first week of release.

Her Majesty is not terribly fond of Buckingham Palace and often resides at Windsor Castle on weekends, holidays and Easter Court. Windsor is where Her Majesty considers home.

1–1 1/2 oz well-chilled Tequilla
lime juice
1 oz well-chilled Triple Sec
salt
Champagne or sparkling wine

Prepare a wine glass (white wine) by rimming the lip of the glass with lime juice and dipping the glass in salt to create a crust. Continue by pouring in Tequila and Triple Sec and stir gently. Top off with Champagne.

Order of the Bath

Also known as Classic Champagne Cocktail

1 sugar cube
2-3 dashes Bitters
Champagne
1 oz Brandy
1 orange slice for garnish
1 Maraschino cherry for garnish

Place the sugar cube in the bottom of a Champagne flute. Use the dashes of Bitters to saturate the sugar cube. Add the Brandy. Fill with Champagne. Garnish with both an orange slice and a cherry.

In 1997, The Queen launched Buckingham Palace's first official website.

Her Majesty is fluent in French and often uses the language to speak with foreign Heads of State, therefore a translator is not required.

1 oz ≈ 30 ml

OBE (Order of the British Empire)

Also known as Savoy 2000 Cocktail

FUN FACT

In June, 2002, The Queen hosted the first-ever public concerts in her private garden at Buckingham Palace to celebrate her Golden Jubilee. The Queen attended both the classical and pop concerts. The 'Party at the Palace' pop concert was one of the most watched pop concerts in history, attracting around 200 million viewers all over the world.

QUOTE

"For me, heaven is likely to be a bit of a come-down"

Queen Elizabeth II

2/3 oz Gin
2/3 oz Melon Liqueur
1/3 oz Limoncello
1–2/3 oz mango juice
Champagne

Prepare a Martini glass by rimming the lip with mango juice and dipping into the granulated sugar to create a sweet crust. Using our shaker, shake together the Gin, Melon Liqueur, Limoncello and mango juice until frothy cold and frosty. Pour into the already chilled frosted glass and top with Champagne.

Golden State Coach

Also known as 170 Cocktail

5 oz Champagne
1 oz Brandy

Simply pour the Brandy and Champagne into a Champagne
flute at the same time, letting the ingredients marry, and serve.

FUN FACT

*Her Majesty has access to
the world's largest collection
of crown jewels but it is her
private collection which is
the most awe-inspiring. The
Queen has inherited some of
the most beautiful jewels in
the world, but has also been
presented with and com-
missioned other pieces as
well. Her Majesty owns the
largest pink diamond in the
world as well as a necklace
with matching earrings of
large square-cut aquama-
rines and diamonds which
were a gift from Brazil.*

QUOTE

"We are not amused"

Queen Elizabeth II

1 oz ≈ 30 ml

Green Park Punch

The Queen and The Duke of Edinburgh were married on 20 November 1947 in Westminster Abbey. The Queen's wedding dress was designed by Sir Norman Hartnell (who was also the designer of her Coronation dress). It was woven at Winterthur Silks Limited, Dunfermline, in the Canmore factory using silk that had come from Chinese silkworms at Lullingstone Castle.

On the morning of her wedding, Her Majesty's bouquet was lost by a footman and her tiara snapped in two as it was being put on her head.

4 oz Champagne
3 oz Melon Liqueur
3 oz Absinthe
2 dashes cherry juice

Before we wash and set the shaker to dry, we have one more task upon us. Fill that shaker one more time with ice, Melon Liqueur, Absinthe and cherry juice. Shake your shimmy and shaker like it is the last dance of the evening and bring the mixture to a frigid froth. Pour the contents from the frosted shaker into an already chilled tall Champagne flute and gently top off with Champagne. Garnish with a slice of honeydew melon and retire to the library, but not before leaving a note that you will clean up in the morning. Enjoy!

Empress of India

Also known as Bubblin' Blue Cocktail

1 cube sugar
1/2 oz Grand Marnier
3/4 oz Blue Curacao

Place sugar cube in the bottom of a wide Champagne flute and dissolve by pouring the Brandy on top. Top off with chilled Champagne and enjoy.

Her Majesty has mastered the art of travel and every mode of transportation there is. She has travelled by horse, carriage, train, plane, boat, subway, tram, trolley and even has her own fleet of Horses, carriages and custom-built, chauffeured Rolls Royces and Bentleys. Until 1997 she had her own private yacht named "Britannia". Her majesty is not solely driven around, she sometimes opts to drive herself to and from events on the royal estates.

QUOTE

"I think everybody really will concede that on this, of all days, I should begin my speech with the words 'My husband and I."

Queen Elizabeth II

1 oz ≈ 30 ml

Diamond Fizz

Also known as French 75 Cocktail

FUN FACTS

Her Majesty has visited the sets of a number of popular British soap operas including Coronation Street, East Enders and Emmerdale.

Her Majesty enjoys impressions, she is said to do a great one of Prince Philip.

2 oz Gin
juice of 1/2 a lemon
1 tsp powdered sugar
top off with chilled Champagne

It should come as no surprise that we will be shaking Gin, lemon juice and powdered sugar in a shaker with ice, which must be shaken until frothy cold. Then strain the mixture into a highball glass over two ice cubes. Continue by topping off with chilled Champagne, give a quick swizzle and serve.

Quotes about Queen Elizabeth II and the Monarchy

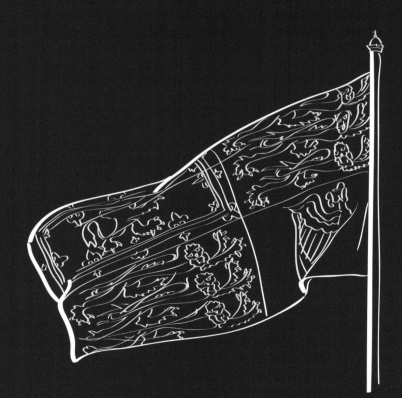

"While there are Presidents in countries all over the world, this country has what some might regard as an anomaly, whereby the Head of State is an hereditary monarch. The greatest achievement of Her Majesty is that she has proved by the way in which she has presided over this country for 60 years that hereditary monarchy provides a better basis for genuine democracy than any of the presidencies …we see in different parts of the world. Her impartiality and knowledgability have demonstrated to all of us that we, who have the best democracy in the world – despite occasional electoral aberrations – owe that democracy, in which all of us are free, to Her Majesty. What she has done in making this United Kingdom a permanent democracy, a democracy that is impregnable, is perhaps the greatest of her many achievements."
Gerald Kaufman MP on The Queen, 7 March 2012

"We have had a Queen who has been able to hold our nation together, and I hope that her life will be long and that, in the years to come, she will be able to hold the United Kingdom together in the way that many of us wish for."
 David Blunkett on The Queen, 7 March 2012

"Selfless, tireless in duty, unflinching in service, unerring in her commitment to the people of Britain, stoical in the face of personal loss, and proud of the extraordinary reach of the monarchy and its values to the Commonwealth."
Ed Miliband on The Queen, 7 March 2012

"According to the UN, seven of the top 10 countries in the world in terms of quality of life are constitutional monarchies."
Rafal Heydel-Mankoo

"The tendency of an advanced civilization is in truth monarchy."
 Benjamin Disraeli

"The monarchy is so extraordinarily useful. When Britain wins a battle she shouts, "God save the Queen"; when she loses, she votes down the prime minister."
  Winston Churchill

"The best reason why Monarchy is a strong government is that it is an intelligible government. The mass of mankind understand it, and they hardly anywhere in the world understand any other."
  William Bagehot

"Anyone who has walked through the deserted palaces of Versailles or Vienna realise how much of a part of the life of a nation is lost when a monarchy is abolished. If Buckingham Palace and Windsor Castle were transformed into museums, if one politician competed against another for president of the republic, Britain would be a sadder and less interesting place. Our politicians are not men such as could challenge more than a thousand years of history."
  William Rees-Mogg

"Honour all [men]. Love the brotherhood. Fear God. Honour the king."
  1 Peter 2:17

"Those who imagine that a politician would make a better figurehead than a hereditary monarch might perhaps make the acquaintance of more politicians."
  Margaret Thatcher

"The Crown is important not so much for the power it wields, but for the power it denies others."
  Sir Winston Churchill

Cocktail Quickfinder

RUM

BRANDY

VODKA

CHAMPAGNE

About the Author

Thomas J.M. Mace Archer DeLacroix Mills

Thomas J. Mace Archer Delacroix Mills is the Secretary General of the British Monarchist Society - an organisation dedicated to defending, protecting and promoting the integrity of the British Crown. He has contributed to such publications as Majesty and Royalty Magazines, Political Pundits UK, The Conservative Blog and Professor David Flints' "An Opinion Column from the National Convenor"– Australia. Having had many works and essays published throughout the United Kingdom and Commonwealth, he no doubt has a superb talent for expressing himself through words.

Thomas, for as long as he, his family and friends can remember, has always had a keen interest in history, politics and monarchy. Always drawing castles, building them out of Lego and blocks; and eventually graduating to studying their architecture along with the residents within, Thomas found a deep-rooted and enthusiastic love of most things Royal. As his Grandfather has served the Crown and his Great-Grandfather before him, he is able to carry on a centuries-old family tradition in serving the crown. Though Thomas may not belong to the Grenadiers in direct service to the Crown, he serves the Crown and his passion through his words, writings and activism in which his defence, protection and promotion of the integrity of the Crown has become more than just a hobby and is now a full-time job with the British Monarchist Society. A somewhat private person, Thomas is a devout and true Monarchist as well as Royalist and sees Constitutional Monarchy as the best performing and most stable form of government in which there is a higher form of governance than that of the politician. He believes there is a higher power, one that is above the pettiness of politics where one can truly be united with his fellow countrymen under one banner that proclaims "For Crown and Country".

Thomas concedes that in today's world, the art of politics is a necessary evil in which there is no true winner on either side from any party. He states that, "Under a strictly political system we can never be one body or one united people as our political beliefs and ideologies pull us apart. However, under an apolitical and higher sense of rule we can truly be bound together under one common body, which is our sovereign who is the embodiment and personification of the state and its people in which an unfailing example exists of what is right and great about our nation". Fully subscribing to the motto of the British Sovereign "Dieu et Mon Droit" (God and my right), Thomas believes that there can be no true kingship without deity and therefore the examples set forth by the Sovereign is in fact one of great balance between moral, religious and social duty. Anglican in his beliefs, he sees the history, meaning and importance of the Crown in the Church as a very relevant and upstanding component of British life as there is a direct correlation to the relationship between the Church, the Crown and the People of these old sceptred isles. Enjoying tradition, heritage and culture, Thomas also enjoys some change and welcomes that which can be beneficial to the rich and deeply-rooted culture that is kept alive and well in our modern British state. He states, "There is nowhere else in the world where the past and present are so intricately intertwined as they are here in Britain and that in itself is something to marvel at as we can still be assured we are the envy of the world when Buckingham Palace is putting on a show, as we have seen over the years with various different events, jubilees and marriages of our Royal House."

British Monarchist Society

The British Monarchist Society is an organisation that meets the needs of the majority in defending their position, which is in favour of the British Monarchy against the moving anarchist's tide of a republican minority. The Crown is important to our unity, stability and peace as a nation. According to the United Nations, seven out of ten of the world's most stable democracies are constitutional monarchies in which the concept of having a non-political Head of State (which cannot be swayed or corrupted) is the greatest safeguard. The sovereign is bound to always act in the interest of their people regardless of the political party in power. The British Monarchist Society welcomes all who support constitutional monarchy and Her Majesty Queen Elizabeth II, no matter where they are in the world.

Teaming with like-minded members of the public, pro-monarchist politicians, celebrities, interest groups, armed forces groups and other monarchist organisations to defend and protect the British Crown, it is our collective duty to ensure our traditions, heritage, culture and values are preserved for future generations. Britain is one of the world's oldest democracies where the constitutional monarch is centred at the heart of this truly unique institution. We are justified in saying freedom wears a crown.

Our reigning monarch, "Her Majesty Elizabeth the Second, by the Grace of God, Queen of the United Kingdom of Great Britain and Northern Ireland and Her other Realms and Territories, Head of the Commonwealth, Defender of the Faith", has devoted her entire life to the peoples of her realms the world over. The Queen is greatly admired and respected for her deep concern and love for her subjects and it is our duty to ensure Her Majesty continues to receive the support and defence she dearly deserves as our sovereign. 'God Save The Queen'.

Diamond Jubilee Anthem

Anton Lorien is a British singer/songwriter whose primary instrument is keyboard/piano. Educated at the British Record Industry Trust School (The Brit School) he made his prime-time television debut to an audience of over 10 million at the age of sixteen. In 2011, Anton released the hit song and music video 'We Are The Brits' for the award-winning charity Afghan Heroes. When asked by the British Monarchist Society to compose a song in honour of Her Majesty's Diamond Jubilee, he put his collaborative album project with a two-time Grammy winner on hold and set about producing the masterpiece 'Like a Diamond'.

'Like A Diamond' was co-written, sung, recorded and produced by Anton Lorien for the British Monarchist Society at the request of Thomas J. Muscatello-DeLacroix Mills who provided much invaluable insight and inspiration. The piece pays homage to HM Queen Elizabeth II as the long-serving leader of our nation and Commonwealth. Proceeds from the download go to The Queen Elizabeth Diamond Jubilee Trust.

'We Are The Brits' is a poignant and uplifting look at the British people and their achievements. Co-written, sung, recorded and produced by Anton; it was written to restore national pride and patriotism and to raise the profile of the charity Afghan Heroes. Proceeds from the download go to Afghan Heroes charity.

"They've done The Queen proud"   *"Inspiring and moving"*
Military Wives Choir   Sir David Jason

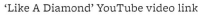

'Like A Diamond' YouTube video link   'We Are The Brits' YouTube video link

Thomas' "Drink" For Thought

I work hard. I slave for my beliefs, to uphold my beliefs and to defend my beliefs. In doing so, I know that I have served a neighbour, a friend, a nation and a crown anointed by the grace of God. In my work I most importantly serve my beliefs. A belief that there is more to a people than the amount of politicians they elect, the laws they impose to shape and direct them, and the amount of taxes they levy for their own benefit. I serve the belief of a higher function of government, a higher power of rule and a higher level of law that can only be instilled through the purity and sovereignty of the Crown. In my beliefs, my work is not easy, defending what I have been called to do – to serve, protect and defend the integrity of the Crown at any cost. On account of all of my passionate and determined hard work, I am most deservedly worthy of a right royal stiff drink!

God Save The Queen!